For THE
COMMON
GOOD

For THE COMMON GOOD

DISCOVERING AND USING

YOUR SPIRITUAL GIFTS

CHRISTINE HARMAN

DISCIPLESHIP
RESOURCES
NASHVILLE

Upper Room Books® website: upperroombooks.com

Discipleship Resources®, Upper Room Books®, Upper Room®, and design logos are trademarks owned by The Upper Room®, Nashville, Tennessee. All rights reserved.

All scripture quotations, unless otherwise indicated, are taken from the New Revised Standard Version Bible, copyright © 1989 National Council of the Churches of Christ in the United States of America. Used by permission. All rights reserved.

Scripture quotations marked NIV are taken from the HOLY BIBLE, NEW INTERNATIONAL VERSION. NIV®. Copyright © 1973, 1978, 1984 by International Bible Society. Used by permission of Zondervan. All rights reserved.

Quotations from *The Book of Discipline* are from *The Book of Discipline of The United Methodist Church—2016*. Copyright © 2016 by The United Methodist Publishing House. Used by permission.

Cover imagery: Shutterstock
Cover design: Ed Maksimowicz
Interior design: PerfecType, Nashville, TN

Print ISBN: 978-0-88177-958-5
Mobi ISBN: 978-0-88177-959-2
Epub ISBN: 978-0-88177-960-8

I dedicate this book to my late mother, Marilou Tapp. She possessed several spiritual gifts, though she would have protested any recognition of them.

Though I was too young to know what it was called, I saw her gift of compassion after she learned of a fellow classmate of mine who couldn't afford weekly milk money. Mom made sure that situation did not continue.

Her gift of exhortation kept me and others moving forward when the path ahead didn't look achievable. Her encouragement always came at the right time.

Her gift of faith sustained her throughout her life. Others would have drawn back from some of the challenges life brought her, yet Mom kept going, confident that God was in control.

While she didn't live to see the publication of this book, her fingerprints are on every page. I could not have done this without her, and I thank God every day for all she brought to my life.

CONTENTS

Preface   9

Chapter One: Why Spiritual Gifts?   13

Chapter Two: Clarity and Relationships in the
    Community of Faith   29

Chapter Three: Identifying Your Gifts   41

Chapter Four: The Calling of the Saints   61

Chapter Five: Expanding Our Profile   73

Chapter Six: Activating Our Gift-Endowed Potential   89

Chapter Seven: Increasing the Impact   105

Notes   125

Answer Key for Spiritual Gifts Inventory   127

PREFACE

I wrote this book not so much to share knowledge and experience but to offer a road map of my daily journey of discovery—the journey that helps me grow in my relationship with God—and to consider what it means to offer that relationship to others within the call God offered me. The signposts of my journey were enlightening for me, and so I encourage you to look for them as you journey through the text.

Signpost #1: God's grace gifts are the province of God to grant. The phrase "spiritual gifts" is unique to Paul's writings, and the Greek word he uses is based in the word *charis*, which means "grace," with the plural of that being *charismata*. This reminds us that all these gifts come from God's grace; and so, it is helpful to think of them as "grace gifts," the unmerited blessings God freely bestows upon us to help us grow in our relationship with God and fulfill our call to discipleship and ministry. Grace gifts are not self-made realities for which we can take credit. Their presence comes solely from the triune God, and they are, in reality, the first equipping tool God extends.

Signpost #2: The granting of these grace gifts has a twofold purpose—one being personal and the other being corporate. On the personal side, the grace gifts we are given enable us to serve God through the uniqueness God granted at our creation. They enable us to live the Great Commandment (see Matthew 22:36-40) and fulfill the Great Commission (see Matthew 28:19-20). On the corporate side, the grace gifts enable us to work for the common good, to band together with others for the betterment of our congregations and the communities in which they are located—our mission field. I have long believed that God has already placed within each community of faith all the grace gifts, skills, passions, and experience necessary for that community to fulfill God's call to mission and ministry in and with its unique mission field.

Signpost #3: There is a dynamic dance of discernment in God's call to us. It is never static but constantly unfolding throughout our lives, and the configuration of our spiritual grace gifts changes along with it. There are times when our call is clear and the direction for its use without doubt. There are also times when we may feel a struggle for clarity and direction, and we question whether God is withholding discernment from us. Those times may offer a unique opportunity if we view them as times of preparation and equipping. The call has already come, and now we see God equipping us in a variety of ways to fulfill that call, with the first act of equipping being the granting of our grace gifts. God is always doing something, whether offering discernment for a distinct means of service or using that time to equip us for what is to come. These are also the times when our personal spiritual practices are crucial in reminding us of our connection to God.

Signpost #4: Love is the universal spiritual gift. In 1 Corinthians 13, Paul refers to several grace gifts and says their presence counts for nothing without our first having love. The word Paul uses for love here is *agape*, the Greek word meaning "unconditional love." It is *agape* love that God has for us; and as with a loving parent, that love is endowed for our benefit but not necessarily for our personal satisfaction at a particular phase of our lives. (The phrases "It's for your own good" and "You'll thank me later" come to mind.) God's *agape* love is what we are called to express toward others for the common good, and our grace gifts are given for the express purpose of doing just that. God has demonstrated love for us and calls us, in turn, to demonstrate that love toward others.

You may discover your own signposts as you journey through this book. Whether you journey with a small group or a class of some kind, I pray you will come to understand your spiritual grace gifts as expressions of God's love and then choose to use them for the love of others—the common good.

CHAPTER ONE

Why Spiritual Gifts?

Concerning spiritual gifts, brothers and sisters,
I do not want you to be uninformed.
—1 CORINTHIANS 12:1

The topic of spiritual gifts has generated much confusion over the years, and with good reason. Perhaps the subject is not taught in some churches because there is no definitive and exhaustive list of gifts that allows us to say *this* is a gift and *that* is not. A survey of available spiritual gifts assessment instruments names as spiritual gifts such things as artistry, celibacy, craftsmanship, exorcism, instrumental or vocal music, hospitality, intercessory prayer, martyrdom, voluntary poverty, and writing. Each one of these is referenced in some part of scripture, and that is how the various assessment tools validate their inclusion among spiritual gifts. In addition, there is no consistency of spiritual gifts inclusion among these various assessment instruments. Some may list a total of ten spiritual gifts, while others may list as many as twenty-five or more.

Hence, an understandable level of confusion is created. And, sometimes, people may shy away from the topic based on experiences they have had with people speaking in tongues or with the interpretation of tongues, two frequently misunderstood spiritual gifts. Perhaps our first step toward eliminating the confusion over spiritual gifts is to set a working definition:

> A spiritual gift is a divine, supernatural ability given by God to enable a Christian to serve and to minister. More simply put, a spiritual gift is a special tool for ministry.[1]

> Our gifts give us the skills and power we need for our specific ministries. When we discover our gifts, we can get a better sense of God's will for our lives and how we can best serve. We are more effective and efficient in our ministry when we use our spiritual gifts. Using our gifts demonstrates the presence of Christ in our lives.[2]

Spiritual gifts flow from God's grace—let us consider them our "grace gifts" (see Romans 12:6).

Why Do Spiritual Gifts Matter to Us and to the Mission and Ministry of the Church?

You may be able to answer these questions before we begin. You may already have knowledge of your spiritual gifts and desire to learn more. Perhaps you know your gifts well and have been serving from them. Or it's possible that you have come to realize your gifts may not always align with a particular ministry in which you are serving in your local church. If you are serving in a civic role in your community, you may seek to better understand how that activity can be a ministry and how you can be most effective in it. However, if you cannot answer the questions, this will be a valuable opportunity to study spiritual gifts and to discover ways to apply them to your life as a disciple of Jesus Christ.

The idea of gifts and gift-giving has long been a part of human history. Let's take a look at the first mention of giving in the Bible. In the first chapter of Genesis, God has completed the tasks of creation, culminating in the blessing of Adam and Eve and issuing to them their first command: "Be fruitful and multiply, and fill the earth and subdue it" (Gen. 1:28). Then, "God said, 'See, I have given you every plant yielding seed that is upon the face of all the earth, and every tree with seed in its fruit; you shall have them for food'" (Gen. 1:29). God explains that this gift is what is needed for sustenance and then goes on to describe how this gift extends to the beasts of the earth. God is the provider of this first gift.

Somehow, though, humanity forgets God's capacity for giving sustenance; and when the Israelites are in the desert during their escape from slavery in Egypt, they start complaining to Moses and Aaron that they are hungry. God, again, gives them what they need. In Exodus 16:9-21, we read the story of God's gift of manna that appeared each morning for the people to consume. This daily gift also came with a miraculous measure: Every person who gathered the bread received exactly what was needed, no more and no less. People who took more than was needed, thinking they might get a head start on the next day's need or afraid God would run out of manna, discovered the next day that the extra measure of manna they had taken had rotted overnight and could not be consumed. Again, God gave the gift of sustenance to God's children, and the human need for food was satisfied by God the Giver.

In James 1:5, we read, "If any of you is lacking in wisdom, ask God, who gives to all generously and ungrudgingly, and it will be given you." We are reminded here that when God gives, it comes as a result of God's being asked. These are just three examples of gifts given from the very heart of God. By studying spiritual gifts, we can rediscover—and reconnect with—the boundless generosity of God's love.

Another reason for your reading this book may be your desire to determine how and where your discipleship can be lived out in service. Unfortunately, the prevailing attitude toward new members of the body of Christ has instead, for many years, been one of assimilating new members into the church, which has often been interpreted as "'put them on a committee." I have been a member of the nominations committee in three different churches, and they all have had several things in common: the task at hand (nominating persons to serve in church leadership positions), the number of meetings and phone calls needed to accomplish that task, and one particular necessary tool for their work. Is that tool the Bible? No. Is it *The Book of Discipline of The United Methodist Church*? No. Instead, it is the most recent pictorial church directory. We on the nominations committee would scan it, looking for people who might be willing to take a particular leadership role in the church for the coming year. Imagine this scenario: A committee is trying to fill the role of Sunday school superintendent, and after suggesting and dismissing a few names everyone knows well, the committee members open the church directory and start scanning it. One person points out a family on one page, and all the committee members recognize that this family comes to worship regularly, their four children attend Sunday school, and they have always attended the monthly potluck dinners. When inquiring what the parents do for a living, they learn that the mother does not work outside the home and the father has some kind of management job. "Let's ask him," the nominations committee members decide. So, page fourteen of the church directory, the second row, third person from the left has provided them with a nominee for Sunday school superintendent. Task done; moving on. When the individual is called later to ask if he will take the job, the responsibilities are explained as being minimal and, therefore, easy enough for virtually anyone to do.

One challenge is that many local churches do not have clear descriptions of the various ministries of the local church. Related to this, we often tend to minimize the expectations for what a good job performance looks like. Do we do this out of fear that people will say "no" if we ask too much of them? To add to the ineffectiveness of this entire process, aside from a very few committees, often there isn't any training offered to help new leaders learn their roles and how to function in them.

Shouldn't there be more than this involved in identifying leaders? In the nominations committees on which I served, it was thought that if we just gave someone a job, all would be well. How many people can you think of in your church who joined the church because they wanted to add some committee roles to their resume? Yet, we still operate as though membership and busyness in or at a local church makes someone a strong disciple.

Compare the above process to this different experience. Another church nominations committee is meeting, and it has a binder filled with printouts. This is a large-membership church with more than 300 slots to fill for the various ministries. Approximately six months earlier, the church leadership team had begun a study of spiritual gifts and how they might be used in congregational life. They decided to initiate a gifts-based approach to identifying, equipping, and deploying lay leadership in the church.

Their first step was to have people take a spiritual gifts inventory. The instrument they had chosen had more than the usual number of gifts and included the gift of hospitality, among others. They had begun distributing these spiritual gifts inventories with their administrative leadership group of nearly fifty persons and then had members of their Sunday school classes and small groups complete the assessment.

From there, they began collecting surveys from attendees of the three worship services. Ultimately, they had collected several hundred completed assessments. The church administrator had input all the data collected into a spreadsheet, then sorted and printed out the results, organized according to each particular spiritual gift. When the nominations committee gets to the group of ministries that includes greeters, ushers, and others whose job it is to extend a welcome to everyone who enters, all they have to do is turn in the binder to the several pages of names and contact information of those who have been found to have a gift of hospitality. While the nominations committee members still have work to do to select people for positions and contact them with an invitation, they know they will be starting with people who are more suited to expressing hospitality and who would be more likely to say "yes," as opposed to making a random attempt at finding someone who might be interested in that particular job.

Church membership is not the same as discipleship. While this seems like a patently obvious statement that should not require debate, the lived-out practice in many local churches has turned it around. Why has this happened? We have spent decades placing an emphasis on tracking how many members a local church has, how many people attend worship, and a variety of other measures. While this data is important, it is far more important to look underneath it to see the true story of a community of disciples living out their call. Are people being taught spiritual disciplines and supported as they try various means of implementation? Do we assume they know how to pray, or do we teach them? Do we spend more time in a new members' class talking about the bygone history of our congregation, or do we talk about the vision to which God calls us? We need to focus more on the spiritual needs of individuals, from cradle to grave, and how the congregation can help people live into the fullness of their discipleship through mission and ministry.

That requires the attention of everyone. All of us are learners on our own unique journey, and, simultaneously, all of us are mentors to those who need support and encouragement on their journey. First, we must help people become established in their role as disciples of Christ Jesus. Then, we can look for opportunities to help them connect their gifts and interests with a ministry that inspires and challenges them.

Discovering and Understanding Our Spiritual Gifts

Think of a ministry group at your church whose members clearly have a passion for what they are doing and each of whom seems to be a perfect fit for the group and its mission. They probably have a dedication to their task and to one another that enables them to keep going, even when situations become challenging. This group is also highly effective and ready to give God the praise for their results. That is what a ministry looks like when the people in it are serving from their giftedness.

Contrast that with a group of people who have said "yes" to a task without having much interest in it. They may have agreed to serve due to a sense of obligation, or perhaps they did not feel they could decline the request. Their outputs are minimal and come with some measure of struggle because no one seems up to the variety of tasks they encounter. There may be internal bickering, and some members may drop out altogether rather than deal with the challenges they encounter. Enjoyment is nowhere to be found. Look inside this group, and you may find that no one's spiritual gifts are aligned with a particular ministry. Please note that there is no guarantee that even the best gift alignment will guarantee stellar results. But what a gift-based ministry approach does offer is the best chance to get the mission and ministry results we desire.

Studying spiritual gifts, learning to work with them, and letting them work for the church can open up and expand fruitful ministry, whether a new ministry or a ministry that has had a long tenure in the local church. When we understand spiritual gifts and how they can be used to fulfill mission and ministry, we can structure the administrative life of the local church in ways that maximize its ministry effectiveness. Recruiting leaders and participants for ministry teams becomes a clearer task and not one people dread, as it helps those who are being recruited to become better-informed decision-makers when they are facing opportunities to serve in their church or beyond. Persons serving from their gifts can experience greater joy in serving, and that joy spills over into the life of the congregation. Implementing various ministries is less arduous, and the results can be more effective.

The spiritual gifts we will examine in this book are not passive in nature. Instead, they are action-oriented and point to a mix of roles and duties. Whether taken together or separately, they have a distinct role to play in building up the local congregation—the body of Christ—and they can impact the community in which that local congregation is located. Many of us discover our spiritual gifts through some kind of assessment instrument and then exercise them through service, all the while growing in the knowledge and love of God through Jesus Christ.

We can also discover our gifts through action. Often, a person's discovery and recognition of his or her own giftedness comes from another individual's observance and experience of him or her. Often, we are able to see the spiritual gifts in someone else, and that observance becomes an education.

Jesus said, "No good tree bears bad fruit, nor again does a bad tree bear good fruit; for each tree is known by its own fruit. Figs are not gathered from thorns, nor are grapes picked from a bramble bush. The good person out of the good treasure of the heart produces good, and the evil person out of evil treasure produces evil; for it is out of the abundance of the heart that the mouth speaks" (Luke 6:43-45). It is not enough just to know our gifts; they must be used. Discovering, understanding, and using our gifts not only deepens our understanding of our relationship with God but also speaks of the authenticity of our discipleship and enables us to respond to our call from God in the most effective ways we can.

Spiritual Gifts and Lay Servant Ministry

The key word in the term Lay Servant Ministry is *servant*, a word of both identity and action. Lay Servant Ministry was never meant to be a title to be achieved for its own sake. Rather, it was designed to be a program of training for disciples to explore God's call in their lives and then live out that call. The variety of Lay Servant

Ministries courses available bears witness to the varieties of spiritual gifts. The content of those courses provides not only knowledge of the course subject but also the tools to explore and employ the use of that knowledge.

This book was written to serve as the primary text for a Lay Servant Ministries advanced course on spiritual gifts. This course is available to and recommended for everyone. If you are pursuing a designation within the Lay Servant Ministries program, it is helpful to take this course at the beginning of your call to Lay Servant Ministry. It can help confirm the direction of your call or it can help you discern the direction in which your call may be taking you. You have been called by God and have been given the grace gifts to live out that call. Sometimes, people believe they first have to achieve a certain level of experience or knowledge to be called by God. They spend a great deal of time trying to "get ready." That also happens frequently in churches where the leaders feel they have to develop their congregation to a certain level before venturing out into the community's mission field. They can end up spending all their time in preparation and never progress toward action.

However, contrary to that mistaken idea about which comes first, the reverse is true: First, God calls; then, God equips. Let's look at a couple of examples, namely Moses and Samuel. The story of God calling out to Moses from the burning bush is likely a familiar one, along with the numerous ways Moses tried to sidestep that call by recounting all his inadequacies:

> Moses said to the LORD, "O my LORD, I have never been eloquent, neither in the past nor even now that you have spoken to your servant; but I am slow of speech and slow of tongue." Then the LORD said to him, "Who gives

speech to mortals? Who makes them mute or deaf, seeing or blind? Is it not I, the LORD? Now go, and I will be with your mouth and teach you what you are to speak."

(Exod. 4:10-12)

God called Moses and then equipped him with all the ways by which God would teach him what to say and how to say it.

Consider Samuel, who was called by God at a young age. Adding to Samuel's youth and lack of experience, his life had been lived outside the knowledge of God: "Samuel did not yet know the LORD, and the word of the LORD had not yet been revealed to him" (1 Sam. 3:7) After Samuel has responded to God's call, we see how God equips him as he grows into maturity: "As Samuel grew up, the LORD was with him and let none of his words fall to the ground. And all Israel from Dan to Beer-sheba knew that Samuel was a trustworthy prophet of the LORD" (vv. 19-20).

To even the casual reader of scripture, it is clear that stories of women in ministry are sparse. Does this mean that God did not call women and then equip them to fulfill that call, as God did for Moses and Samuel? No. It does mean, though, that the language of call must be interpreted from the text, since it is not specific. Let's examine the story of Lydia, in Acts 16. She is obviously a worshiper of God, since Paul encounters her at a prayer gathering on the sabbath. We can conclude that God's call to Lydia had come at some point in time prior to this. The moment of equipping for her came when "the Lord opened her heart to listen eagerly to what was said by Paul" (v. 14). God equipped Lydia to listen and respond to the message Paul was bringing and to consider ways to use her social and economic position to support Paul's mission. From that time on, we see Lydia's ministry begin to flourish. She had her entire household baptized; and, since there was no synagogue in the town, her home became the meeting place for believers. Lydia's ministry of hospitality to fellow believers made her the planter of the first house church in Europe.

As we serve from our spiritual gifts, we discover more about God, ourselves, and our relationship with God. We can gain a deeper understanding of the priesthood of all believers. As stated in *The Book of Discipline of The United Methodist Church—2016*, "All Christians are called through their baptism to this ministry of servanthood in the world to the glory of God and for human fulfillment" (¶126, "The Heart of Christian Ministry"). The purpose of our call has two directions. It is first directed toward God and for God's glory. It is also directed toward our fellow human beings to enable humanity to live its fullest potential with the abundance Jesus spoke of in the Gospel of John (see 10:10). The writer of First Peter put it this way:

> Like good stewards of the manifold grace of God, serve one another with whatever gift each of you has received. Whoever speaks must do so as one speaking the very words of God; whoever serves must do so with the strength that God supplies, so that God may be glorified in all things through Jesus Christ."
>
> (1 Pet. 4:10-11)

In this passage, we do not see a listing of spiritual gifts but rather a division of the diverse gifts into two categories: speaking and serving. Paragraph 128 of *The Book of Discipline* reinforces this call: "All Christians are called to minister wherever Christ would have them serve and witness in deeds and words that heal and free." Again, we see the vehicle for serving: "deeds and words." What we do should reflect what we say, and what we say should give rise to what we do. Therein lies integrity.

I spent twelve years working in a management position at a bank where the annual performance appraisal included two exercises separate from the supervisor's input. One exercise was to submit a listing of performance goals for the following year, which was a great opportunity to set a course of activity that related to corporate goals and objectives. The other exercise was to state self-assessed weaknesses and present a plan to overcome them. While I made legitimate efforts to follow those plans, the whole process seemed counterproductive and felt frustrating to me: What if I failed to turn those negatives into a positive? The time I had to spend creating a plan and then seeking remedies to the negatives seemed to take my energies away from doing the job I was hired to do. I am not saying I was without flaws, but I often had difficulty seeing where this activity was going to benefit anyone, including me. After all, I thought, if my very nature was problematic, why was my employment continued and awarded with increasing responsibilities and regular salary increases? This yearly routine was not as mentally rewarding nor as inspiring for me as the goal-setting phase. As it turns out, there may have been a good reason why.

There is a frequently used group exercise in which participants are asked which hand is dominant. Then they are told to place their pen or pencil in the opposite hand and write their name. The results are predictable and so are the participants' responses to the exercise: "It was harder"; "It took more time, and I had to really concentrate"; "I can't read my own name." This exercise is a lot like being told to create a plan to address personal weaknesses and expect monumental achievements: Why focus on the negative when the positive can more easily get the job done with far better results and leave us feeling better about our efforts? Why not work from the positive?

Part of my current job involves being part of a group of coaches for congregational revitalization. I have worked with local congregations for nearly twenty years and can say it is a different experience to start discussions with what a church does well rather than what problem needs to be fixed. When we approach the church as a problem, the conversation is sometimes depressing, sometimes angry. Blame is at the heart of every negative incident cited. Body language and facial expressions reflect dissatisfaction and, sometimes, surrender.

Contrast that with congregational conversations that focus on the positive, and you will see that the energy in the room is different. People smile as they recall and name the good moments in their congregational life and history when things have gone well and the church was filled with life. They laugh at some of their recollections and sometimes become emotional as they narrate their deepest moments of faith, love, and respect for one another. Later, they are far more creative in the challenge to build upon what they already do well as opposed to finding some tool to "fix" what is wrong with them.

To fine-tune that initial discussion, the question is not just what a church does well, which could be barbecues or potluck dinners. Rather, the question is often, "When have you felt the congregation was most alive, inviting, and effective in ministry in your community and beyond?" Other questions might be, "Tell me about a time when this congregation was living its greatest obedience to God"; or "Tell me what this church is like when it most reflects Jesus to the community." As you may well imagine, when these are the questions we ask, we hear stories from people that bring smiles to their faces as they recall the positive, God-directed aspects of their congregational life, as opposed to the frowns when speaking of what is wrong.

To apply this on a personal level, think about what it is like for someone to tell you a story of the best time in their life. Now, imagine, if you will, what the dialogue would be like if you were to ask someone, "When have you felt closest to Jesus?" The response would be stories that enable us to see what touches the individual most personally and what can be an impetus for further spiritual development and growth in sanctifying grace, the grace that comes as we live our lives, maturing in our discipleship.

How Will We Proceed?

Chapter one has been an overview of the topic of spiritual gifts and the reasons for studying them and considering possible applications. The examination of spiritual gifts that follows in this book will be anchored in scripture, especially key passages from three books of the New Testament—Romans, First Corinthians, and Ephesians. It will include researching additional scriptures to gain further depth of understanding of these gifts. Therefore, as you continue reading this book, be sure to read the corresponding texts noted for each chapter and any further references. We will not only examine what has been written about spiritual gifts but also place it within the context of the location, its people, and the times.

Chapter two will examine the issue of clarity about the subject of spiritual gifts and address the role of our relationships with other people.

Chapter three will offer the opportunity to identify our own spiritual gifts, along with definitions and ideas for them in scripture.

Chapter four will explore God's call in our lives and the issues or needs that touch our lives. This call is one that beckons our gifts and ignites our passions, resulting in a vision for service.

Chapter five will help us round out our understanding by delving into the resources we have at our disposal—our abilities and skills. It will also address the life experiences we have had and look at how our personalities shape our response to the world around us.

Chapter six will address ways we can grow in sanctifying grace through our giftedness and how active participation in the functions of fulfilling the mission of the church helps us mature in our faith.

Finally, chapter seven will present ideas for how a local congregation can employ a system of gifts identification and use it for leadership development and greater effectiveness in its mission and ministry, both for those within the membership of the church and for those in its community—the mission field.

Using This Text in a Lay Servant Ministry Class

Participating in a ten-hour Lay Servant Ministry advanced course will enhance your learning about spiritual gifts and their application for the glory of God. For that purpose, there is an accompanying leader's guide available separately for purchase that offers exercises and activities, along with questions for individual reflection. It includes opportunities to share those thoughts with others in a class learning experience or study group and to explore new questions as well. This Lay Servant Ministry advanced course could also be adapted for use in an adult Sunday-school setting by taking one chapter each week (or spread out over two weeks) and using the corresponding learning activities in the course leader's guide.

May God's blessings go with you as you learn and explore and not only discover your spiritual gifts but also realize opportunities to use them for the common good and for the glory of God.

CHAPTER TWO

Clarity and Relationships in the Community of Faith

To each is given the manifestation of the Spirit for
the common good. . . . For in the one Spirit we were
all baptized into one body—Jews or Greeks, slaves or
free—and we were all made to drink of one Spirit.

—1 CORINTHIANS 12:7, 13

Have you ever heard someone say, "My spiritual gift is patience"? Or perhaps, "My spiritual gift is joy"; or possibly, "My spiritual gift is kindness." As fine as these attributes are, they are not typically considered spiritual gifts, at least not in the writings of Paul we will address in this book. They are, however, listed in Galatians 5:22-23—along with love, peace, generosity, faithfulness, gentleness, and self-control—as being part of "the fruit of the Spirit." These qualities are often confused with spiritual gifts. It is not uncommon for some persons, when asked what their gifts are, to respond with some aspect of the fruit of the Spirit. This is not to say, though, that there is no relationship between fruit and gifts. They were both endowed to human beings by the Holy Spirit. The fruit may be evidenced in how a particular gift is lived out. For example, a person may have the gift of shepherding and exercise it with patience and gentleness, two traits that are the fruit of the Spirit.

Still others may claim as a gift something not listed in scripture at all. Things such as playing a musical instrument, being a great cook, and being available to drive people to the grocery are great abilities and characteristics to have and can be useful in various ministries, but they are not included in Paul's comments as being spiritual gifts. Are there other spiritual gifts that are not indicated in Paul's writings in the New Testament? That is a good question and a distinct possibility. However, we will devote our examination of spiritual gifts to those that are listed as such in Paul's writings.

Another phenomenon we can see in today's church is that of categorizing one's spiritual gifts as some kind of personality- or psychological-type test that renders a particular result. Whether it is the preferred learning-styles test ("I'm a visual learner"), the DiSC behavior assessment ("I'm an *S*"), the Enneagram personality-type assessment ("I'm a 6"), or Myers-Briggs ("I'm *ISTJ*"), we carry the result as a label and a shortcut to understanding ourselves or dealing with other persons. As beneficial as these tests can be for their intended purposes, their primary emphasis is on the individual, with some correlation to the individual's relationships with others. The purpose of knowing our spiritual gifts, on the other hand, is to discover where they can best be employed for the common good as we live in the interconnectedness of relationships in the body of Christ.

While we can point to any number of misperceptions about spiritual gifts in the church today, these are not a new issue. In the apostle Paul's time, the church at Corinth was in upheaval over a number of things, including spiritual gifts. To understand Paul's explanation of spiritual gifts, we need to become somewhat familiar with the city of Corinth, its people, and the contextual issues affecting that world. Examining context will help us place the rationale for Paul's communicating what he did. Paul's first letter to the Corinthians addresses a variety of issues he anchors in a reframing of the basic theology of Christian believers. Those issues were born of the city of Corinth and its culture, history, and peoples.

The city of Corinth, in our narrative, is located on a narrow isthmus that connects two bodies of water. Because of the location, it is a crossroads of commerce and travel, and therefore a segment of the population has become wealthy. The people who come through Corinth and those who settle there are a mixed lot from multiple countries of origin, beliefs, and practices. There are numerous temples there honoring a wide variety of gods, including Greek, Roman, and Egyptian.

The growing number of believers in Corinth are those who have heard and embraced Paul's preaching and witnessing that Christ is the Messiah. As other people are converted, they also share the gospel, and the number of believers increases. At the end of this passage, we see that Paul travels to Ephesus. It is later, while he is in Ephesus, that he receives a letter from the Corinthian believers, referred to in 1 Corinthians 7:1. Apparently, in this lost letter, the believers raise a number of issues regarding the behaviors of members of the church. We can conclude that many of them have been having difficulty letting go of their former lifestyles in this city, ranging from idol worship to sexual immorality. In his response to them, Paul refers to some of their points of concern. To understand all of this and, in turn, Paul's teaching on spiritual gifts, we need to establish the context of the letter and the underlying issues of the people to whom he is writing.

When Paul composes his letter to the Corinthian church, he has a particular purpose in mind—that of speaking to the divisions that have arisen in the young church that are evidenced in their letter to him and correcting faulty views and practices among the believers. As the book of Corinthians opens, Paul says that word has reached him of quarrels among the members of the Corinthian church. Apparently, these quarrels are based upon whose baptism they have received: baptism from Paul, from Apollos, from Cephas, or from Christ. This is why Paul clarifies his purpose as being to proclaim Christ and not to baptize.

Since the Corinthians have become somewhat elitist around a variety of issues, especially wisdom, he also spends some time downplaying the importance of human wisdom. Perhaps this fascination with wisdom has come from Greek influences, as this has been a key issue among Greek culture, with the goddess Athena being the goddess of wisdom, among other things. The church members' appreciation and validation of this kind of wisdom is what Paul feels he needs to rectify. The "wisdom" of a Greek goddess, as such, is not the wisdom that will sustain them as a people and as a church, Paul implores; the wisdom that comes from the Spirit is what is valid.

Paul goes on to school the Corinthian church members as to the pettiness of these quarrels. After all, he says, they are not acting as though they are spiritually mature. In fact, he refers to them as spiritual babies, not even ready to consume solid spiritual food. Their squabbles and jealousies are keeping them in the flesh and, therefore, incapable of understanding the things they want most to understand. Paul's charges are meant to be a kind of wakeup call for the people of Corinth: Stop the disagreements and start acting like spiritually mature believers.

Over the next few chapters, Paul addresses the issues of sexual immorality; lawsuits; marriage; singleness; sacrifices; head coverings; and a few others, for good measure. All of this comes before Paul begins his teaching on spiritual gifts, and we can see from the breadth of his instruction that the Corinthian church certainly has need of some instruction on a wide variety of issues. Woven throughout Paul's comments regarding the Corinthians' behavior is his theological teaching of the foundational principles of the faith.

Questions about spiritual gifts are next on his agenda; and when we look at the whole of First Corinthians, we cannot help but notice that this topic is given three chapters of attention (chapters 12 through 14). This is quite a lot of space for one subject. Let's look back at 1 Corinthians, chapter 1. Paul has first stated a reminder that the members received God's grace through Jesus Christ and that they have been enriched in everything. He then says, in verse seven, that the reason for this has been "so that you are not lacking in any spiritual gift as you wait for the revealing of our Lord Jesus Christ." This is key information. It is not that spiritual gifts are foreign to the Corinthians; they just need to be reminded that they already have what they need and that those gifts are distributed throughout the body of believers and not granted to just a handful of persons. Apparently, though, through their beliefs and practices, they have misconstrued how those gifts are given and how they are to be lived out. For example, a key issue among the people of the church at Corinth has been regarding how some have been given the gift of speaking in tongues and have considered themselves far superior to other persons because of that gift; this had been taken for a handy, and public, way to set themselves apart from the general population.

This is why Paul begins the twelfth chapter of 1 Corinthians by saying he does not want people to be ignorant about spiritual gifts. (*Hint:* They already are.) What he has heard about their practices, perhaps from the questions raised in their letter to him (and possibly in the earlier "lost" letter), may have communicated to Paul some kind of ignorance on their part that he feels needs to be corrected. He affirms to them the power of the Holy Spirit as the grantor of these gifts and that it is only by the power of the Spirit that people can confess, "Jesus is Lord."

Paul then sets up a three-part explanation of spiritual gifts (vv. 4-6). First, he says that there are, indeed, different spiritual gifts, yet it is this same Spirit that grants them. This is a way of saying that all gifts come from the Holy Spirit and are, therefore, all valid. Second, Paul speaks of different ministries or "services," but he says that these too relate to the same Lord. Third and finally, Paul says there are different activities (some translations say "results"), but it is the one God who produces them. This all-encompassing treatment of the spiritual gifts serves to diffuse some of the Corinthians' attitudes toward gifts, including their belief in some of the gifts having such great stature when compared to the others that they must come from a different source. Not so, says Paul. The gifts are given to each individual for a particular purpose: that they be exercised "for the common good." This phrase is a key part of Paul's teaching. The gifts are not there for a few individuals to set themselves apart from others by boasting in their possession. The gifts are not to divide the community but, rather, to unite it. This common good is focused on all people as a means of helping them. Practicing any spiritual gift for a different purpose defies the purpose for which God endowed that gift through the Spirit.

By emphasizing this common good, Paul underscores the issue of unity while honoring the diverse ways in which people can use their gifts for that purpose. Just as there are numerous gifts, there are also a variety of ways to use those gifts. While the scripture does not say so, we can assume that in order for people to use their Spirit-given gift, they do not have to do this apart from other persons. Very often, when an individual's gift is combined with the gifts of others, the effect is magnified beyond what any of us could do individually. The result is far greater than the sum of its parts. That is testament to the greatest power coming when we function in an interconnected relationship with others. Gifts are given to enhance the connection and result of a unified body of believers. Contrary to what some of the members of the Corinthian church believed, those with the gift of speaking in tongues were not set apart as a privileged class of believers and, therefore, exempt from God's purpose.

Unity

Staying in the twelfth chapter of First Corinthians, there is a passage that may be familiar to you; it is often the subject of sermons and is taught in a variety of settings. In this passage, Paul uses the human body as a symbol of the kind of unity that is needed in the young Corinthian church but which they are not living out at that time. What may not be well known, however, is the fact that this metaphor of the human body was not original to Paul. Instead, it was a common metaphor, having one point of origin in a Greek fable attributed to Aesop (620–564 BCE). Centuries later—but still well before Paul's time—the Greek philosopher Plato, drawing upon earlier influences, would use the image of the body in his work the *Republic* (c. 375 BCE). And historians in the Roman Empire used the body metaphor to describe the relationship between the people and the empire's system of governance: Every demographic classification of people had a function in service and relationship to the whole of Roman society through its government's structure and goals.

When the Corinthian church members read this part of Paul's letter to them, the allusion to a body is a familiar basis for teaching and understanding. It is familiar territory that both the writer of the letter and the receivers can follow and understand. This passage also includes a lot more than may at first meet the eye. In it, Paul chooses to address the growing breakdown of unity among the believers. He drives home the point that all are necessary for the one body to be whole by pointing out the folly of the notion of the body being just an eye or just an ear; consider what would be lost, he asks of them.

The recipients of this epistle had a lot of issues to deal with, and some of these issues were based in pride. The social competitiveness of the people in Corinth was a serious influence that compelled some members of the Corinthian church to place themselves above the other members. The general culture of the city of Corinth fed this kind of class stratification, with some of the moneyed class considering those of lesser financial means to be beneath them—and, therefore, without any power and reason for the upper class to consider them at all. Paul understood this, and so, within the body metaphor, he made direct points against anyone claiming to be better: "The eye cannot say to the hand, 'I have no need of you'" (12:21). Just as foolish as this statement would be, Paul says, so is it folly for one group of people to be so assured they know the mind of God that they would unilaterally dismiss any persons based upon what they alone perceive regarding their relative worth to society.

It is unfortunate that some people think they have no gifts at all and may feel they have nothing to contribute. Scripture refutes this idea. Spiritual gifts come from the Holy Spirit, and every believer receives at least one (see 1 Peter 4:10). Some people have gifts that are frequently used "behind the scenes," so they may not consider these gifts to be significant; yet, without them, various efforts fail for lack of precisely this kind of support.

Paul continues on to say to the Corinthians that what they think may be lowly and unnecessary may ultimately be given the highest place of honor. This message of not trying to second-guess God's purpose for individuals echoed Christ's message of the last being first and the first being last. This was all for the purpose of reminding the Corinthian church that unity is crucial and that the interdependence of every member is to be the hallmark of the community of faith. In 1 Corinthians 12:12-31, Paul uses the word *all* thirteen times. His message is clear: There is to be no segregation or stratification among the members. We could say that Paul was preaching unity as a basic value of the Corinthian believers.

It is helpful to remember that Paul's letter to the Corinthians was a continuous narrative. It did not have the divisions we recognize as chapters, although our analysis relies upon those segmentations. When Paul finishes what is denoted as chapter 12, he has been addressing speaking in tongues and their interpretation. He again downgrades the relative importance of these two gifts, so prized by some members of the Corinthian church, by saying in chapter 13 that they are worthless if they do not come from love.

This also carries over to other acts of the believer, as the absence of love makes the possession of other gifts hollow and worthless.

Paul's description of what *love* is sets the foundation for a healthy spirituality that is observable in the behaviors of the believers. He instructs them as to what love is and how it behaves. He contrasts what behaviors are the antithesis of love, and he is very specific about them. Again, this correlates to his needing to address the negative behaviors that had been reported to him and that were becoming commonplace in the church at Corinth.

Chapter 14 then continues with an extensive teaching on speaking in tongues, its proper use, and its comparison to the gift of prophecy:

> I would like all of you to speak in tongues, but even more to prophesy. One who prophesies is greater than one who speaks in tongues, unless someone interprets, so that the church may be built up. (v. 5)

Prophecy was foundational, according to Paul, in its ability to teach, encourage, and support people; whereas, speaking in tongues was limited in its ability to apply Spirit-led truths to the general population of believers. When speaking to the gathered believers, Paul says, the assembly can serve as an accountability agent for what is shared in prophecy.

Additionally, for the gift of tongues to edify the body, there must be someone available to interpret what is being said. Otherwise, it does not help anyone but simply calls attention to the one speaking. Here, again, is an emphasis on the whole community as the priority, instead of the elevation of or admiration for any one person, and Paul includes himself. Again, the teaching of this chapter serves to underscore the nature of interrelatedness among the believers and their accountability for strengthening those relationships.

While we will be examining the ways spiritual gifts can be used in service, let us not forget or take for granted the fact that our spiritual gifts are directly linked to our relationship with God through Jesus Christ. They are given by God through the Holy Spirit, and each gift is given for a purpose—that of strengthening our unity and living in relationship with one another for the common good. Coming to understand our own spiritual gifts is crucial to understanding our call to Christian ministry.

By gaining clarity about spiritual gifts, we can, like Paul, dispel the misunderstandings and misperceptions regarding the topic. Doing so will help place spiritual gifts within their proper place—being seen and understood as endowed by God through the Holy Spirit and recognized as having specific purposes in God's kingdom.

In the next chapter, we will determine our own spiritual gifts and explore what each one means.

CHAPTER THREE

Identifying Your Gifts

We have different gifts, according to
the grace given to each of us.
—Romans 12:6, NIV

The book of Romans, written during Paul's third missionary journey, is regarded as his most thorough and complete treatment of his theology. He addresses numerous issues, including salvation through Christ and sanctification. Paul's letter is addressed to both Jews and Gentiles in the Roman church, and Paul lays out his discussion with clarity and efficiency.

In the first eleven chapters of his epistle to the Romans, Paul has been teaching and explaining his positions on a variety of issues. In the first verse of chapter twelve, we find the word *therefore*. Here, Paul is emphasizing that what came before is foundational to what will come next. Anytime we see or hear the word *therefore* in scripture, we should consider it an arrow that points to something important about to be said or read. At this point in his letter to the Romans, the primary doctrine narrative has concluded, and Paul is moving into the life-application phase of his writing.

In this passage Paul also returns to his analogy of the human body. He is preparing the recipients of the letter to see the relationship between gifts and their usage—just as it is the job of the eye to see and the ear to hear. Body parts have different functions, and so do we, as we recognize and use our gifts. As he did in his letter to the Corinthian church, Paul emphasizes the importance of each person and makes the point that all are necessary. He calls the Roman church members to respect the diversity of the spiritual gifts and their functions.

In this chapter, our purpose is to determine which gifts have been given to us. Later, we will note the skills and/or abilities we have along with these gifts. This will enable us to begin focusing on how God has made each of us and God's loving act of gift giving through the Holy Spirit. This first step will lay the foundation upon which we will build a profile that can guide us into fulfilling God's call into mission and ministry.

Please note that this inventory—and others like it—is not definitive as to whether an individual possesses a gift or not. There is no statistical foundation upon which to say a particular score means the gift is present or not present. This is merely a tool that can be used to measure the strength of presence of a particular gift in an individual at a particular time. God can bring a seemingly minor gift to the forefront, depending upon the situation and the particular call of that individual. Our spiritual gifts can also change over time, as our experiences continue to shape our lives.

Read through the statements within each group. Then, score each statement as to how true you believe those statements to be for you at this time. Use the scoring system below. Then, total each group of statements, and record your score. (Your score for each group of five questions should range between 0 and 15.)

3 = Almost always true of me
2 = Sometimes true of me, about half the time
1 = Rarely true of me; rarely happens
0 = Not ever true of me

The corresponding answer key is found on page 127 in the back of this book.

GROUP A   My score: _____

____ I believe God has used me as an instrument of healing.

____ Most of my prayer time is spent on behalf of people who need healing.

____ There have been times when God has sent God's healing power through me to help other people.

____ I believe God still heals people, just like the stories in the Bible tell us God did.

____ People have told me they felt a healing presence when I prayed for them.

GROUP B   My score: _____

____ It is easy for me to determine whether or not someone is authentic in their spirituality.

____ I am able to detect false teaching.

____ I can tell when someone's ministry is driven more by a desire for recognition and attention than a desire to serve God humbly.

_____ I am able to tell when someone is speaking out of an inspiration of God.

_____ I can tell the difference between someone who is moved by the Holy Spirit and someone who is acting out of their own motivations.

GROUP C   My score: _____

_____ I place a high priority on getting tasks done quickly and correctly.

_____ I am comfortable working behind the scenes to support the community of faith.

_____ I feel close to God when I am doing routine or ordinary work in the church.

_____ There is no task too trivial for me if it helps build up the body of Christ.

_____ I enjoy getting a job done for the sake of getting it done, and it doesn't matter whether I get recognition or not.

GROUP D   My score: _____

_____ In my deepest prayer experiences, I speak to God in words I don't understand.

_____ I often speak in tongues when I feel the power of the Holy Spirit most intensely.

_____ The first time I prayed in tongues, it came very naturally to me.

_____ When offering praise and thanksgiving to God, I often feel that common language is inadequate.

_____ Praying in another language, perhaps an unknown language, has had a great impact upon my prayer life.

GROUP E   My score: _____

_____ I never tire of doing in-depth study of scripture to make it easier for others to understand its lessons.

_____ I am thrilled to see another person grow in knowledge and understanding of scripture.

_____ I am more comfortable creating my own teaching material than using mass-prepared material.

_____ I am able to explain scripture in a variety of ways so people can understand it.

_____ I am able to use various delivery methods in class to adapt to the diversity of learning styles.

GROUP F   My score: _____

_____ I would be willing to go wherever Christ calls me to start a church.

_____ I would jump at the chance to relocate to serve the church and bring new believers to Christ.

_____ I have a strong desire to take the gospel to an unchurched area.

_____ I am comfortable with people of diverse cultures and backgrounds.

_____ I would be comfortable sharing the gospel with persons whose beliefs and culture are different from mine.

GROUP G   My score: _____

_____ I am blessed to be able to give money for the mission and ministry of the church.

_____ I know God will meet all my needs and that I can therefore share my income above and beyond my tithe.

_____ I practice giving as a spiritual act of gratitude offered to God.

_____ I make sure my offering goes to my church each week, even though I may not be physically present.

_____ I believe giving 10 percent of my income to the church is just the starting point of my stewardship.

GROUP H   My score: _____

_____ I believe God is as active today as in biblical times.

_____ I know that I can trust God's promises no matter what else may happen around me.

_____ I firmly believe trusting in God will make all the difference in a person's life.

_____ I see God's presence in all aspects of life today.

_____ It is especially meaningful to me to be able to spend a lot of time praying on behalf of other people and their situations.

GROUP I   My score: _____

_____ I have interpreted tongues to help other people worship God.

_____ I am able to detect whether or not someone is authentic when that person is speaking in tongues.

_____ When I hear someone praying aloud in tongues, I know exactly what that person is praying.

_____ If someone is speaking in an unknown language while in a state of spiritual ecstasy, I am able to interpret to others what is being expressed.

_____ I believe unbelievers can be helped when I interpret speaking in tongues in a worship service.

GROUP J   My score: _____

_____ I do not shrink from sharing biblical truth, even though I know I might be criticized for doing so.

_____ I believe God gives me special insights into building up the body of Christ.

_____ I am able to point out to people how they should change their lives to grow closer to God.

_____ I often feel compelled to share spiritual insights that I believe God has given to me specifically.

_____ I am able to show others how God's word speaks to today's situations.

GROUP K   My score: _____

_____ I have often been moved by God to offer good advice when asked for my opinion about a particular situation.

_____ When I have offered counsel regarding spiritual matters, people have told me I demonstrate spiritual maturity.

_____ I am frequently able to see how God's truth applies to specific situations.

_____ At times, I have demonstrated a kind of wisdom that can only come directly from God and not from my own experience.

_____ When there are several positions on an issue, I have a strong sense of which direction God wants taken.

GROUP L   My score: _____

_____ I am effective in getting a group of people to complete their assigned task and celebrate their achievement.

_____ People often look to me as an example or role model.

_____ I am good at figuring out who the best person is to get a job done and then delegating the work to that person.

_____ I am good at stating a large goal, then helping people figure out ways to organize themselves and get it done.

_____ If I am part of a group that is disorganized, I will step forward to help them get organized.

GROUP M   My score: _____

_____ I am thrilled to be able to lead others to Christ.

_____ I believe winning people to Christ is the most important thing I can do to serve God.

_____ My heart is burdened when I think of those who have not made a decision for Jesus Christ.

_____ I never tire of telling people what a difference Christ has made in my life.

_____ I am comfortable in sharing the gospel of Christ with unbelievers.

GROUP N   My score: _____

_____ I feel compelled to help people in need and find I am more blessed for doing so.

_____ I seem to be able to see where people are hurting and where they need comfort more quickly than others do.

_____ I have a strong desire to reach out to those who are in need (physically, spiritually, and emotionally).

_____ I seem to spend some part of each day responding to someone in need, even if it is just listening.

_____ I feel very close to Christ when I am able to reach out to people who are disadvantaged or neglected.

GROUP O   My score: _____

_____ I am personally well organized, and when I set a goal, I follow through to achieve it.

_____ People frequently turn to me to help get something organized.

_____ I am able to remain calm in chaotic situations and focus on the action necessary to achieve a goal.

_____ I can help people identify their gifts and abilities and then assist them in finding ways to use those gifts and abilities to serve God.

_____ I feel greatly rewarded when I can help get a project organized and see people functioning to accomplish the goals of the project.

GROUP P   My score: _____

_____ I have been used by God to turn what seemed impossible into something that was possible.

_____ I have been a tool in God's hands to bring about supernatural changes in people's lives.

_____ I have felt prompted by God to do something for God and have seen unexplainable results occur.

_____ I have seen God work miracles through my prayers.

_____ God has used me to make something happen that was beyond human capability.

GROUP Q   My score: _____

_____ There have been occasions when I have received powerful insight into a situation by some means other than normal communications.

_____ At times, I have been speaking to someone and become greatly aware of something happening in that person's life, without their telling me about it.

_____ There have been times when I suddenly understood particular choices open to the church when no one else did.

_____ God has enabled me to know something before other people became aware of it.

_____ People have been surprised when I tell them something about themselves that they did not share with me.

GROUP R   My score: _____

_____ I enjoy guiding people on their spiritual journey.

_____ People know I have a genuine interest in seeing them grow as disciples.

_____ People often turn to me for spiritual guidance and direction.

_____ I am willing to take responsibility for helping a group of people develop Christian maturity.

_____ I take very seriously the call to nurture people in the development of their faith.

GROUP S   My score: _____

_____ I am always willing to do something for people to free them to serve in their own ministries.

_____ I know that my service behind the scenes is necessary to enable more visible things to happen.

_____ I enjoy working in the background in ways that help other people get the spotlight focused upon them.

_____ I receive great joy in serving the church in ministries that enable other ministries to happen.

_____ People know I can be counted on to think of the small tasks that need doing and that no one else usually thinks about.

GROUP T   My score: _____

_____ People often turn to me when they are feeling down and need encouragement.

_____ I seem to be able to offer trusted counseling without sounding like a know-it-all to people who turn to me.

_____ I enjoy coaching others in their spiritual growth, especially when they are encountering problems.

_____ I never tire of offering encouragement to other believers.

_____ I believe it is important for me to help others see how God works in their lives, even in the tough times.

Definitions

The following definitions and scriptural references will offer information about each spiritual gift. Some will also offer instruction for their use, and others will provide inspiration by example. For each spiritual gift, there is also a suggested corresponding hymn from *The United Methodist Hymnal.*

Administration—The ability to organize and coordinate people and other resources for the effective implementation of various ministries. Administration is a versatile gift, as most ministries need someone with organizing abilities to help turn plans into reality. It usually involves organizing multiple resources, including people. Its presence enhances other activities, and most groups or committees realize their actions need administration to be effective. Administrative help makes a lot of ministries flow more smoothly. (See Luke 14:28-30; Acts 6:1-7; Romans 12:28; and Titus 1:5. Hymn #433, "All Who Love and Serve Your City.")

Apostleship—The ability to introduce the gospel of Jesus Christ to new people and then nurture the development of their faith. The gift of apostleship does not mean all attempts will be successful. Paul, who described his calling as an apostle, encountered many situations in which he and his message were not met with open arms. There remains a need for apostleship in today's world. We are most likely to see its need in emerging cross-cultural ministry opportunities. We are likely to see apostleship at work with evangelism, reaching out to our mission fields. Keep in mind, those mission fields do not have to be far from home; they are, essentially, the world beyond the doors of our local church, the world we see every day as we go about our normal lives. (See Acts 1:1-5; 15:1-2; 15:22-23; 2 Corinthians 12:11-12; Galatians 2:1-10; and 1 Timothy 2:7. Hymn #568, "Christ for the World We Sing.")

Compassion/Mercy—The ability to sense the pain or suffering of others in ways that compel one to take action to alleviate their condition. *Compassion* should not be confused with having *pity* on someone. The primary difference between the two terms is that *compassion* obliges action, as exemplified in the story of the good Samaritan; and *pity* is an attitude we may take when we see or hear of someone suffering or experiencing distress. (See Matthew 9:35-36; Mark 9:41; and Luke 10:33-35. Hymn #355, "Depth of Mercy.")

Discernment—The ability to distinguish between the things of God and those not of God to strengthen the body of Christ. In the listing of spiritual gifts, this gift is referred to as "discernment of spirits." Another example describes being able to distinguish false teachers. Those with this gift can help people not fall victim to charlatans. Persons with this gift are highly sensitive to other people's attitudes and can "hear between the lines" of what other people may say, both positive and negative. Their level of understanding enables them to be a voice for people unable or unwilling to express themselves and their ideas. Those with this gift need to remember the purpose of this gift is to strengthen the body of Christ and use that as a guideline for where and when to share the things they have discerned about others. (See Acts 5:1-11; 8:22-23; 2 Peter 2:1-3; and 1 John 4:1-6. Hymn #601, "Thy Word Is a Lamp.")

Evangelism—The ability to communicate the gospel to unchurched persons in ways that move them to become disciples of Jesus Christ. Evangelism can be both the personal sharing of the gospel of Jesus Christ and the witness a congregation makes before its community by the things it prioritizes and how it lives out its mission as a community of faith. While we all promise to bear witness to the life, death, and resurrection of Jesus Christ, those with the gift of evangelism possess the rare ability to reach people in ways that result in a profession of faith. They understand that while faith-sharing is not a complicated issue, its dedicated practice is a way of life. Many people seem to shy away from personal evangelism due to a faulty perception of what it means to be an evangelist but not people with this gift. (See Acts 8:26-40; 14:21; and 1 Corinthians 3:5-7. Hymn #584, "Lord, You Give the Great Commission.")

Exhortation—The ability to offer encouragement to those who are disheartened and may be struggling in their faith. Even small acts of encouragement can make a difference in people's lives. Many people can recall, sometimes from many years prior, how one person offered words of encouragement that enabled them to continue. People with the gift of exhortation offer unending support and encouragement to others, caring about another person's self-confidence and development. This encouragement is usually directed at the individual's devotion and obedience to certain principles, values, or beliefs. Sometimes called "balcony people," those with this gift are life's cheerleaders, faithful supporters of others in their walk with Christ. (See Acts 14:21-22; 1 Timothy 4:13; 2 Timothy 4:1-2; and Hebrews 10:24-25. Hymn #117, "O God, Our Help in Ages Past.")

Faith—The ability to depend upon God's promises with steadfast belief and certainty that God will accomplish God's purposes. Faith is at the heart of Christian living as it is expressed in love and action. It is more than our basic statements and professions of faith; this gift takes faith to an exceptional level. Persons with this gift are likely to have a deep and profound prayer life, and they live in daily assurance of God's promises—those realized and those yet to come. This is another one of the enhancing gifts that extends to other gifts and ministries. (See Matthew 17:19-21; Mark 9:23; Acts 11:22-24;

Romans 4:18-21; Ephesians 2:8; and Hebrews 11:1-30. Hymn #452, "My Faith Looks Up to Thee.")

Giving—The ability to manage one's personal resources (money, time, skills, and energy) to joyfully contribute more than expected to the church and its ministries. In the story of the poor widow who gave two coins, Jesus teaches us that giving does not require great assets but rather a faithful and loving heart. Persons with this gift are able to give due to their practicing sound personal management of their resources. They do not give to every request, realizing that some requests in the world are not legitimate. Instead, they do not hesitate to probe into where their giving will go and how it may be sustainable. (See Mark 12:41-44; Acts 4:32-37; Romans 16:1-2; and 2 Corinthians 8:1-5; 9:2-7. Hymn #399, "Take My Life, and Let It Be.")

Healing—The ability to be an agent through whom God restores health and wholeness to people who are ill. An active prayer life for the healing of someone can also be an act of trust in God's power to heal, whether the individual experiences healing or not. Those with the gift of healing realize that theirs is not the kind of ability that Christ practiced in the Gospel texts. Rather, they realize that the healing comes from God and that its culmination may and often does take a variety of forms at any given time. Notice that in First Corinthians 12:9, when discussing healing, the text says "gifts" (plural). All the other gifts are noted in the singular. This may indicate that our understanding of healing should take a variety of forms and that, therefore, we would expect to see a variety of results. (See Acts 3:1-10; 5:12-16; 9:32-35; 28:7-10. Hymn #375, "There Is a Balm in Gilead.")

Helps—The ability to provide assistance to others for a release from their worldly or spiritual burdens. The gift of helps is more than pitching in to lend aid; the acts are directed at alleviating encumbrances. People with the gift of helps are those tireless workers whose presence makes things go better. They are always at the ready to respond and do so with a cheerful heart. This is another enhancing gift whose offerings cross all lines of ministry and help round out the effectiveness of other gifts. (See Acts 9:36; 20:35; and Hebrews 1:14; 6:10. Hymn #634, "Now Let Us From This Table Rise.")

Interpretation of tongues—The ability to translate and reveal to the body of believers the message shared by someone speaking in tongues. Paul had very specific instructions for this gift, in relation to those who speak in tongues. So important is this gift of interpretation that without the presence of an interpreter, those with the gift of tongues should remain quiet. (See Acts 2:1-13; and 1 Corinthians 14:1-14, 27-28. Hymn #539, "O Spirit of the Living God.")

Knowledge—The ability to understand or comprehend the truth of a situation or belief from God's point of view. When shared with others, it is observed as wisdom. Modern viewpoints consider this to be related to knowledge in general and an ability to gather information and synthesize it into concepts. This approach is closely correlated with personal learning styles. (See Colossians 1:9-12; 2:2-3; and 2 Peter 1:2-11. Hymn #420, "Breathe on Me, Breath of God.")

Leadership—The ability to share God's vision and will for the church and its people, then to inspire and direct them to accomplish God's will. The gift of leadership can be expressed in a variety of places and does not always have to be at the top of the organizational chart. A poorly led support committee can have detrimental effects, but a well-led one contributes to the church's mission. This is another enhancing gift that applies across all ministries in the church and, when done effectively, enables achievement of desired results. The gift of leadership focuses on the places God desires people to go and functions in ways that inspire people to follow toward that destination or vision. Without leadership, ministries may fail in their execution, and people may become frustrated and withdraw their participation. (See Acts 7:9-10; and 1 Timothy 3:1-13. Hymn #128, "He Leadeth Me: O Blessed Thought.")

Prophecy—The ability to relate biblical truth in timely and relevant ways that offer interpretation of historic or modern messages from God. In some scripture passages, this may be translated as "preach" or "preaching." The gift of prophecy is applied to presenting situations; it does not serve as a kind of fortune-teller, seeing into the future. It is common for modern-day prophets to be dismissed or ignored if their statements call us to recognize we have strayed from God's will. (See Acts 2:14-36; 11:27-30; 15:30-33; and Ephesians 3:1-6. Hymn #159, "Lift High the Cross.")

Serving—The ability to provide service or labor to support the mission and ministries of the church. These acts can be ordinary or routine and performed in a way that is often unnoticed. Those with the gift of serving put the needs of others ahead of themselves. We take our example from Christ, who took the role of a servant and washed the feet of the disciples. (See Acts 6; Galatians 5:13; 6:10; and Titus 3:14. Hymn #581, "Lord, Whose Love Through Humble Service.")

Shepherding—The ability to nurture, tend, and lead people in the ongoing development of their discipleship. The gift of shepherding

applies to both pastors and laypersons who care for the congregational flock. Shepherds care for the advancement of the group in
their care while seeing to the individuals within that group. This
ministry is vital to those who guide covenant discipleship groups
or other small groups for ongoing discipleship formation. (See
Matthew 18:12-14; John 10:11-18; Acts 20:28; and 1 Peter 5:1-4.
Hymn #381, "Savior, Like a Shepherd Lead Us.")

Teaching—The ability to analyze, communicate, and apply biblical
truths and other Christian teachings in ways that help people grow
in faith. The gift of teaching is not limited to Sunday school activities. There are many other opportunities to apply this gift, both
inside and outside the local church. The gift of teaching requires a
lot of work by the one who has the gift, as the teacher must also be
a continual learner. Effective teachers not only know the facts but
also know how to convey them in ways that learners can understand and translate into the behaviors of a disciple. (See Acts 18:24-
28; Colossians 3:16; and James 3:1. Hymn #277, "Tell Me the Stories
of Jesus.")

Tongues—The ability to pray, praise, or speak in an unknown or
foreign language. Refer to "Interpretation of tongues" for instructions regarding when to share this gift publicly. (See Acts 2:1-13; and
1 Corinthians 14:1-14. Hymn #539, "O Spirit of the Living God.")

Wisdom—The ability to make exact and practical applications of
knowledge imparted directly by God. The gift of wisdom works
well with the gift of knowledge. Knowledge provides the "what to
do," and wisdom offers the "how." Those with the gift of wisdom are
the ones we seek to create responses to various situations, as well
as test solutions we may already have determined. The counsel of

those with the gift of wisdom is sought by leaders and shepherds, seeking to be their most effective as they relate to people within their span of care. (See Acts 6:3-10; 1 Corinthians 1:18-27; 2:6-13; Colossians 1:28; 3:16; and James 3:13. Hymn #598, "O Word of God Incarnate.")

Working miracles—The ability to perform supernatural acts that transcend our understanding of nature's laws. The gift of miracles is not only about being used by God in ways we cannot predict or understand but also about living in ways that demonstrate our belief that God does, indeed, work miracles and that we *expect* God to work miracles. Any actions in which the gifted individual is engaged are done in ways that point to God and not to the individual. (See Acts 4:29-30; 9:36-41; 20:7-12; and Romans 15:18-19. Hymn #57, "O For a Thousand Tongues to Sing.")

CHAPTER FOUR

The Calling of the Saints

*I therefore, the prisoner in the Lord, beg you to lead a
life worthy of the calling to which you have been called.*
—EPHESIANS 4:1

Now that you have assessed the current strengths of your
spiritual gifts, this chapter will consider the call of our gift-
empowered future. It is in this stage that we will think about our
gifts and ask ourselves, *What if?* The stories you share of instances
when God's gifts were being most clearly expressed in your life give
clues to the call or vision that beckons you forward. There is a strong
relationship between God's call and our gifts. God's call is typically
encased in some kind of vision that offers direction or a degree of
specificity. Yes, we are called, and that call is to a vision of ministry.

Where, then, does God's call beckon us? First, it calls us to live in
an ever-increasing love and knowledge of the triune God. Second,
it calls us to discern the particular vision God has for us. Let us
think of *vision* as a picture of a future reality. Our work of discernment, then, is to seek God's guidance as to what God envisions for

us. That vision may be something exciting or it may inspire fear; I suspect it is usually a little of both. In any case, it is God inviting our called being into a picture of need that will serve the common good. We are called to God's vision for each of us.

Consider Mother Teresa as an example of this. She was first called by God to set her life apart as a Catholic nun. Later, the vision emerged of how she might best use her life—by ministering to the poor of Calcutta.

An ordained clergyperson receives a call to ministry. Later, that call is directed toward the vision of a ministry dedicated to social justice.

A layperson responds to a call to serve God by becoming a Certified Lay Minister but is not sure how or where that service should be lived out. Then, the vision begins to emerge of what that service would look like, and it enables that person to refine and focus his or her service.

The call to God's vision may be revealed at the outset. It may also evolve as a kind of call within a call. Either way, God sees a picture of where our capacity can be leveraged to meet a need and endows us with spiritual grace gifts to meet that call toward vision fulfillment.

Paul does not debate whether or not someone was called. After all, he had experienced his own call on the road to Damascus (see Acts 9). Later, his call was affirmed to others in the church at Antioch when the Holy Spirit said to the prophets and teachers assembled there, "Set apart for me Barnabas and Saul for the work to which I have called them" (Acts 13:2). In his letter to them, Paul states that those in the Ephesian church have indeed been called, and his comments speak to them from that position. Several scriptures reference God's call to the believer: First Corinthians 1:2; 7:17;

Ephesians 4:1; 2 Timothy 1:9; and 1 Peter 2:9-10. In these passages, Paul clearly gives church members a reminder that being a believer and accepting God has called them are forever linked: One cannot be a believer without understanding that it carries with it the acceptance of a call.

"The Call to Ministry of All the Baptized"

Paragraph 220 of *The Book of Discipline of The United Methodist Church—2016* begins as follows:

> All members of Christ's universal church are called to share in the ministry which is committed to the whole church of Jesus Christ. Therefore, each member of The United Methodist Church is to be a servant of Christ on mission in the local and worldwide community. This servanthood is performed in family life, daily work, recreation and social activities, responsible citizenship, the stewardship of property and accumulated resources, the issues of corporate life, and all attitudes toward other persons. . . . Each member is called upon to be a witness for Christ in the world, a light and leaven in society, and a reconciler in a culture of conflict. Each member is to identify with the agony and suffering of the world and to radiate and exemplify the Christ of hope. (¶220, "The Call to Ministry of All the Baptized," 2016 *Book of Discipline*)

When we accept the fact of God's envisioned call in our lives, some questions may arise: *I am called but to what? What does that mean, and how will that enable me to "radiate and exemplify the*

Christ of hope"? Our questions of where, what, how, and for whom we are to be "a servant of Christ on mission in the local and world-wide community" are natural inquiries. To answer those questions, we need to examine the various ways in which we live and live out that call. Furthermore, we must consider both those in which we are currently engaged and those toward which God is calling us.

Expressing Servanthood Through Family Life

According to the Social Principles of The United Methodist Church, "We believe the family to be the basic human community through which persons are nurtured and sustained in mutual love, responsibility, respect, and fidelity" (¶161B, *The Book of Discipline of The United Methodist Church—2016*). Each week, we are exposed to teachings of the gospel at church; and when we leave the building, we have the next six-and-a-half days to live out what we have learned. As with any learning process, it is in the practice of that learning that we grow and through which growth is reinforced by support and the sharing of examples. It is also a responsibility of parents to "train children in the right way, and when old, they will not stray" (Prov. 22:6). Family life is where our servanthood can be expressed through worship, faith formation, and ongoing reflection on God's Word.

Expressing Servanthood Through Our Daily Work

Many of us may spend as many—or more—waking hours in a day in our work environment as in our home. We bear witness to Christ in how we conduct ourselves with our coworkers and how we handle the stresses of deadlines and changing task assignments. A firefighter I know lives his faith in the fire station, and it continues when the alarm sounds; he is praying while he and his fellow firefighters are *en route* to the site of the call. His prayers continue during those times when he uses the Jaws of Life to extract someone from a crashed vehicle. He doesn't preach a sermon—he lives it.

Expressing Servanthood Through Our Recreation and Social Activities

Our social lives may give us a glimpse of our character, and it is here that our faith behaviors are on display for all to see. Someone has said, "Sport doesn't build character. Sports reveal it."[1] The United States loves its sports, and church leagues are popular across a variety of sports. A friend of mine once shared a story of how his love of sports and his competitiveness called him to a powerful and painful realization and, ultimately, a change in his discipleship. During one season, he had exhibited a hot temper that increased in severity and frequency with each passing game. He attributed it to his passion for the game and promised himself he would not let the pressures of the game get to him. During one game, however, his competitiveness got the better of him, and he lashed out at what he considered to be a bad call. He was embarrassed by his behavior and realized that he had not kept Christ with him when he began to play. He confessed this sin to God and promised that it would never happen again. And it did not. It did, however, drive home a powerful lesson in how easily people can deny Christ by putting something else first in their lives.

Expressing Servanthood Through Responsible Citizenship

There is an unfortunate tendency to segregate our "church life" from our "civic life" by claiming that civic engagement is not something the church should engage in because that means politics. Yet, the issues that challenge citizens living in our communities also affect those same citizens when they attend church on Sunday morning. Those challenging issues also confront persons not attending any church; these are the people of our mission field, and if they are hurting or suffering from systems of injustice, we are called to step up. John Wesley and his brother Charles had been visiting imprisoned persons, seeing to them and their spiritual needs early in the Methodist movement. Their experience brought them the realization that they should be reaching out to persons affected by injustice. Micah 6:8 speaks to us: "He has told you, O mortal, what is good; and what does the LORD require of you but to do justice, and to love kindness, and to walk humbly with your God?" The scripture doesn't say, "Only on Sunday" or "never outside of church"; there is no separation.

Expressing Servanthood Through Stewardship of Property and Accumulated Resources

The Book of Resolutions and *The Book of Discipline* state the following:

> All creation is the Lord's, and we are responsible for the ways in which we use and abuse it. Water, air, soil, minerals, energy resources, plants, animal life, and space are to be valued and conserved because they are God's creation

and not solely because they are useful to human beings. God has granted us stewardship of creation. We should meet these stewardship duties through acts of loving care and respect.

(¶160.I., "The Natural World")

That care and respect should be extended to our personal resources. We are a nation of over-consumers, and so great is our obsession with owning things that many cannot contain all their possessions in their primary residence. According to industry statistics, the self-storage business brings in nearly $40 billion a year in rental income, and there are more self-storage units than there are McDonald's and Starbucks locations combined.[2] When it comes to stewardship, downsizing is becoming a spiritual issue.

Issues of Corporate Life Offer Opportunities for Servanthood

It is within our communities of faith that the culture of our discipleship is formed and exemplified. The corporate mission and ministries of a local congregation speak to the community, and members of that congregation have the responsibility for communicating that message. Each one of us is a representative of our local church and a living advertisement for the attitudes and practices of that church. Perhaps we need to rediscover the practices of the early church expressed in Acts 2:44-47:

All who believed were together and had all things in common; they would sell their possessions and goods and distribute the proceeds to all, as any had need. Day by day, as they spent much time together in the temple, they broke bread at home and ate their food with glad and generous hearts, praising God and having the good-will of all the people. And day by day the Lord added to their number those who were being saved.

While the realities of life in the early twenty-first century do not compare with this passage, we can still take lessons from the practices described and translate them to the modern day. Most people typically do not live in a commune; but when there is need in the community, so often, they respond as though they are one. For example, after a natural disaster occurs in a small community, people respond with a unity that binds them together. By way of another example, many churches collect gently-used clothing for distribution; many also offer clothes closets along with their food-pantry ministry. That practice is one example of distributing assets to those in need. What other ways might your congregation live a lifestyle congruent with the guiding words of Acts 2:44-47?

Expressing Servanthood in Our Attitudes Toward Other People

"May the God who gives endurance and encouragement give you the same attitude of mind toward each other that Christ Jesus had" (Rom. 15:5, NIV). Paragraph 162.III ("The Social Community") in the Social Principles begins this way:

The rights and privileges a society bestows upon or with-holds from those who comprise it indicate the relative esteem in which that society holds particular persons and groups of persons. We affirm all persons as equally valuable in the sight of God. We therefore work toward societies in which each person's value is recognized, maintained, and strengthened.

"Do nothing from selfish ambition or conceit, but in humility regard others as better than yourselves. Let each of you look not to your own interests, but to the interests of others" (Phil. 2:3-4). Christlike attitudes and practices hold all persons in esteem, yet the issue of racism and the language of hate still exist in the United States and beyond. Such language, attitudes, and actions are incompatible with Christian teaching and cheapen our witness. While we may not say such things ourselves, any time we say nothing when a racist or culturally demeaning joke is told in our presence, we have cheapened our witness and failed in our servanthood. "If any think they are religious, and do not bridle their tongues but deceive their hearts, their religion is worthless" (James 1:26).

Where Is Our Best Place of Servanthood?

This call to ministry of all the baptized spans a great variety of venues and relationships, and they all need attention. An individual may find himself or herself drawn to a particular area because it seems to be the one area most in need of devotion and attention. That may be the very place to which God is calling that person. People frequently find themselves living out a ministry they had never envisioned, one that leads them to say something such as, "If anyone had told me five years ago I would be doing this, I would have said they must be thinking of someone else." That unplanned place of ministry may be the place where God sees a need and is calling you to step in to fulfill it.

Responding to God's call to ministry is not the prescription for satisfying our own personal—and, sometimes, selfish—needs. After all, the gifts have a twofold purpose: They serve us in our own spiritual development, and they also are to be directed for the common good. That common good is defined from God's perspective. This is true not just for people in today's church. Consider Moses, who tried every tactic he could think of to avoid God's call as it came to him from out of the burning bush. Whenever Moses would offer an excuse, God would counter with a response to overcome it. Similarly, it is not uncommon for people today to describe their response to a call to the ordained ministry by recounting all the reasons and excuses they had given for saying "no."

What Brings Enthusiasm to Your Call?

Chariots of Fire is a film that tells the story of two British track athletes competing in the 1924 Olympics. One is Jewish; the other is Christian. The Christian is planning to be a missionary to China, and his sister sees his training for the Olympics as a conflict and distraction from his preparing to be a missionary. He speaks with his sister and allays her concern by telling her he knows God made him for the purpose of being a missionary to China. He continues to tell her that God also made him fast and how when he runs, he "feels God's pleasure."

The place where we feel that same pleasure is the place that reveals our vision, heart, passion, or dream. It is the thing that stokes our emotions, and our response to it is emotional. That emotional response then feeds our motivation to act. It is the people, places, issues, or concerns that spark our interest and compel us to do something. Those places are the desire God has placed in our hearts; and laboring within that desire is satisfying and fulfilling, even though, at times, it may be difficult.

By way of example, the number of children in the United States who do not have enough to eat is surprisingly high, with more than 11 million living in what is termed "food insecurity."[3] Schools may have free lunch programs, but when those children leave school on Friday, they have no guarantee of getting anything to eat until they come back on Monday. There are many programs that seek to do something about this, and they are growing across the country. In one such program, healthy food and snacks are donated and put into backpacks for the children to take home. That seemingly small amount of food can make a difference for that child. When one asks volunteers why they do this, one hears stories of the heart of those volunteers being touched in such a way that evokes an emotional, heartfelt response. That response then turns into action.

Think about your normal day and the people with whom you interact. How many times do you hear the phrase "I just *love* . . ."? What usually follows can be a name, a movie, a song, a meal, a vehicle, a book, and so on. Yet, as much as we may care about such things, I daresay most of them probably would not rank among those things that could motivate a lifetime pursuit.

What provides that motivation for you? Clues may be found in experiences that gave you the greatest feeling of meeting another person's needs. Sometimes, being able to offer the one thing someone needs can bring great joy. Often, it is the situation itself that touches us, even though we are not currently doing anything about it. For example, if you are watching or listening to a news report online or on television, does something you hear cause your ears to perk up? Do you read a story about a situation affecting a group of people and say to yourself, *If only I could do something about it?* What is it you envision doing?

Ask those who know you well to tell you what they believe you care about most. Their responses may surprise you. They may have noticed something you said or did that was memorable to them, even though it may have been something so small that you did not think about it. Nonetheless, it struck a chord in the observers, and they thought your behavior was expected for who you are. What we are known for is the message our lives and behaviors sends to others, consciously or unconsciously. There are two factors that intersect. One is what we say; the other is our actions. What we believe and say should compel our actions, and our actions should point to what we believe. This evidences an authentic discipleship that brings our God-given gifts together with our passions and ignites our action. In faith, we cannot help but respond.

Knowing our gifts adds insight into our call and shapes how we live it out through a variety of arenas. The more we know about where our interests lie and the situations that speak to our passions, the better able we will be to direct the fulfillment of our call to mission and ministry within our local congregation and beyond. Spiritual gifts and the vision of our call to ministry intersect and reinforce each other. Our gifts can affirm our vision, and our vision can be enhanced by seeing God's gifts as being in support of it. This kind of alignment also enables congregations to direct the gifts and ministry interests of their members toward fulfillment of the mission of the church: to make disciples of Jesus Christ for the transformation of the world.

In the next chapter, we will round out this picture by considering other elements that have an impact on how we use our spiritual gifts and how we seek fulfillment of our vision for ministry.

CHAPTER FIVE

———

Expanding Our Profile

*Speaking the truth in love, we must grow up in
every way into him who is the head, into Christ,
from whom the whole body, joined and knit together
by every ligament with which it is equipped,
as each part is working properly, promotes the
body's growth in building itself up in love.*
—Ephesians 4:15-16

S o far, we have examined our call as disciples and determined our spiritual gifts, realizing how vital is the link between God's vision and the particular configuration of gifts God has bestowed. We see that, while the call remains the same, the configuration of gifts can take different forms as conditions change and opportunities arise. As we live our lives in a growing love of—and obedience to—God's call, we find ourselves navigating life's changing landscape. We may realize an increasing clarity of that call as we learn which things draw forth our interests and skills and which things detract. Our life priorities change. We learn to move away from the detractions and toward those strong influences that deepen our faith and refine our choices regarding how we live that faith.

This is exciting, as it allows us to begin putting some specificity to what we have discovered and the purpose toward which we desire to direct it. This is where we create a challenging plan to synthesize what we have learned in our discoveries and stated in our vision by building out an expanded profile. In bringing the gifts God has given to the vision God has revealed to us, we can expand our understanding toward a plan for practical living. We can begin to live into the fullness of our call to ministry.

The power of this phase of building is that it will create a personal infrastructure that compels us to actively seek its fulfillment. Upon completion of the build phase, you will have a better understanding of the many ways God has blessed your life and continues to bless it. Just as God gave the Israelites manna in the desert, God's grace has given you all you need to be in ministry as a disciple of Jesus Christ. Taken together, this picture will bring greater clarity to how you view your life, its experiences, and your call to the future.

While the description of this building phase may sound like a linear activity, it is, instead, an organic one. Building from what you have discovered and the dream you have claimed, it is now that we will add other elements that propel us toward a ministry based upon our particular spiritual gifts. This will enable us to see how our gifts and other aspects of our human existence work together to paint a picture of our calling and our potential to fulfill that call.

This infrastructure can take numerous forms, so we will look at several models and compare their common elements to assist you in finding a model that works for you. The first model is called S.H.A.P.E., and it was developed by Rick Warren of Saddleback Church.[1] Reverend Warren is the author of *The Purpose Driven*

Church and *The Purpose Driven Life.* This model has become well known and is used by a variety of churches across the country, largely due to its simplicity and ease of understanding, as well as the books published and conferences presented by Saddleback. The model can be found in Baptist, Methodist, and Presbyterian congregations, to name a few, and many other models have been developed from it. The S.H.A.P.E. acronym is easy to remember: **S**piritual gifts, **H**eart (passions, what energizes the individual), **A**bilities (skills the person possesses), **P**ersonality (preferred styles of working and approaching tasks), and **E**xperiences (life lessons that can contribute to shared realities). The training on the model begins with a question: How has God shaped you for ministry? What is most impressive is the system they have instituted for using the model in ways that help everyone find their best fit for ministry and, thereby, help the church and those it serves.

In the Saddleback system, members take a series of four-hour classes, and one of them has participants work through the process of discovering their "shape." After that, persons who are trained as "shape counselors" sit down with the individuals and look at their responses. They compare those responses to a series of profiles of ministry and service opportunities in the church, and together, they select one to try.

More recent models are interpretations of or variations on this basic design. For example, Church of the Resurrection (COR) in Leawood, Kansas, has used a model they called S.T.R.I.D.E., which stands for **S**piritual gifts, **T**alents, **R**esources, **I**ndividuality, **D**reams, and **E**xperiences.[2] In this model, the leaders work with participants in an eight-week small-group study. At the conclusion of those eight weeks, participants can opt for a personal conversation with a ministry-placement consultant to help them narrow down their choice of ministry service.

In Matthew 20:28, Jesus said, "The Son of Man came not to be served but to serve." Jesus later demonstrated his teaching on servanthood by girding himself with a towel and taking the role of a servant to wash the disciples' feet. This is the basis of another model called G.I.R.D., which stands for **G**ifts, **I**ndividuality, **R**esources, and **D**reams.[3]

Here (with some necessary rearrangement of the categories) is a comparison of the three models we have examined. Let's examine these common elements. Of course, spiritual gifts are a basic

	S.H.A.P.E.	S.T.R.I.D.E.	G.I.R.D.
Spiritual Gifts	✓	✓	
Gifts			✓
Heart	✓		
Dreams		✓	✓
Ability	✓		
Talents		✓	
Resources		✓	✓
Personality	✓		
Individuality		✓	
Individuality (includes experiences)			✓
Experiences	✓	✓	

requirement of each model, and since we have explored gifts in a previous chapter, we will look at the other elements here.

Dreams (passion, heart, vision)

This component deals with an individual's aspirations—something he or she would like to be part of and contribute to its accomplishment. Saddleback calls it "heart," with both the S.T.R.I.D.E. and G.I.R.D. models calling it "dreams." (We began our look at this in the last chapter.)

This element is crucial in that it provides the spark that ignites commitment. It is the cause or need in the human condition that touches the emotions in people and leads them to say, "I must do something about this." The chance to change someone's life or right a wrong can also inspire others to join in that work. It can keep people engaged in an activity when technical challenges arise and "when the going gets tough." This is the thing that sustains people in working longer hours and committing more of their personal assets to the fulfillment of the cause. It is the tug they cannot ignore; it is the motivation from within.

Resources (abilities, talents)

Saddleback Church's S.H.A.P.E. model refers to this category as "abilities," while the S.T.R.I.D.E. and G.I.R.D. models call it "talents" or "resources." Whichever the choice of term, this element adds a fullness and richness to our call and puts muscle to our gifts.

In Genesis 1:26, God speaks of the creation of humanity and includes the pronouncement that humankind will "have dominion" over the animal kingdom. In that pronouncement, it is implicit that

God's design of humans included the ability to *act*. We can see this in the verbs God uses in the Genesis Creation story: "Be fruitful and multiply, and fill the earth and subdue it; and have dominion" (Gen. 1:28). At the point of call, God is bidding people to use their resources and abilities to activate their response.

Let me pause a moment to point out that while the terms *skills* and *abilities* may seem interchangeable, there is a distinction between the two words. *Abilities* are usually considered to be the natural capacities one possesses, while *skills* are those things that are acquired by other means. In many ways, a person's acquisition of a certain skill set is due to an innate ability that is foundational to that skill set. For example, an individual may possess the ability to empathize with another person. After attending a training class on communication skills for caregiving ministries, that person is now equipped with the skills for having a caregiving conversation with someone experiencing grief.

We are all offered the choice to bring our spiritual gifts, our abilities and skills, and our vision together with God's call in our lives and turn that result into action. Choosing to ignore our personal capacity is to walk away from a God-given opportunity to show our gratitude to God and represent Christ in the world.

This element relates to all the skills you possess and exercise during any given day, and it would probably surprise you to learn just how many skills you actually use. Also, there are specific skills related to a particular task or field of work. For example, think about some of the skills needed to do laundry.

- Sorting items ensures that they get the right temperature of water and spin speed.

- Assessment skills are needed to determine whether an item may bleed color and thus need to be washed separately, with special handling.
- Accurate measuring of detergent ensures items are clean without causing suds to overflow out of the washing machine.
- There may be a second sorting when it comes to determining which items go into the dryer and at what temperature those items should be set to dry.
- When the dryer completes its cycle, another assessment is performed to determine whether anything needs to be ironed. If ironing is needed, a determination must be made as to what temperature to set the iron.

Sorting, assessing, deciding: These are just a few of the skills needed to perform the mundane task of doing laundry. What skills are needed, then, to prepare a meal, offer basic first aid, create a budget, read a map, or balance a checkbook? Daily living requires particular skill sets; some are complex, and some are simple. Yet, we all go through our days using the skills we possess in our lives and careers.

It has been estimated that an average adult may possess up to 700 unique skills and abilities.[4] Does that surprise you? If it does, it is probably because we do not consider all the "micro-skills" we employ as part of routine living. Just as assessing whether or not a garment requires ironing is itself a skill, as we read in the example above, we may have been more likely to consider the entire operation of "doing the laundry" as one skill, when, in fact, it was a series of several smaller skills, each one necessary and connected to all the others.

When thinking about skills or abilities, we frequently believe we have to be an expert at a particular skill. That is not true. We can possess any number of abilities and skills without being an expert in them. Creating a budget is a skill that does not require a PhD or an MBA in finance or accounting. Neither does one have to be a world-class chef to cook a hamburger; rather, preparing that burger is a skill that is made up of a lot of smaller skills, such as shaping the burger, determining if the pan or grill is hot enough, and testing for doneness, just to name a few.

Hopefully, the differences between abilities and skills have become more apparent by now. First, some of these abilities come naturally to us, so we can say we are born with some abilities. We may think of the so-called "natural athlete"; or have you ever known anyone who could play virtually any song on a piano or other instrument "by ear," without having formally studied music?

Second, many skills are best honed outside any formal-education arena. Apprenticeships are the hallmark of many skilled trades, and they are effective for a reason: On-the-job training engages a person in context-based work that cannot be adequately described in a book or demonstrated in a classroom. A seasoned mentor with a watchful eye can coach the apprentices as they practice their new skills.

To help you begin thinking about all the possible skills or abilities you may possess, let's examine a few categories and partial lists of what may be included.[5] Note that the items in these lists are all verbs, and thereby they are able to be ascribed to any particular field of work or life without being bound by context. You may find some skills listed in both sections, as some skills can be considered both physical and intellectual. For example, one could mentally interpret something being read and then physically (verbally) interpret that information to another person.

Interpersonal/physical abilities and skills: *add, adjust, advise, align, allocate, apply, appraise, arrange, assemble, balance, bind, blend, build, calculate, calibrate, change, choose, clean, collate, collect, combine, connect, coordinate, construct, control, correct, counsel, count, create, crush, cut, decant, defend, demonstrate, diagram, dilute, discard, dismantle, dispense, dispose, dissect, drain, draw, dry, employ, erect, estimate, evacuate, examine, execute, expel, facilitate, fasten, fill, filter, fix, frame, freeze, gather, grade, grasp, grind, group, guide, handle, heat, identify, illustrate, incubate, inject, input, insert, inspect, install, invert, investigate, isolate, justify, label, lay out, locate, localize, maintain, make, manage, maneuver, manipulate, mark, measure, mediate, mix, moisten, mount, negotiate, note, observe, obtain, open, operate, overhaul, pack, perform, persuade, place, plate, plot, position, pour, prepare, press, process, produce, program, pull, puncture, push, read, record, release, remove, repair, replace, retest, rinse, roll, rotate, save, scan, score, screen, seal, select, separate, set, sever, shake, sharpen, ship, siphon, sketch, sort, spin, spread, squeeze, stain, standardize, start, stick, stir, stop, store, suspend, take, test, text, thaw, thread, tilt, time, tip, trim, touch, transfer, troubleshoot, turn, type, use, utilize, view, warm, wash, watch, weigh, withdraw, wipe, wrap.*

Knowledge-related/mental abilities and skills: *advocate, analyze, appraise, approve, arrange, assess, associate, audit, brief, budget, calculate, choose, cite, clarify, classify, commit, conclude, confirm, consider, convert, criticize, critique, define, decide, depict, describe, design, develop, diagnose, differentiate, discriminate, distinguish, endorse, envision, evaluate, examine, explain, forecast, formulate, identify, infer, inform, instruct, integrate, interpret,* *interview, investigate, itemize, judge, justify, label, list, match, name, organize, outline, plan, prescribe, prioritize, prove, question, rank, rate, reason, recall, recite, recognize, recommend, recall, recognize, record, recount, reorder, repeat, report, research, resolve, revise, rule on, select, solve, state, support, synthesize, tell, transmit, translate, validate, verbalize, verify, write.*

Let's look at what God says about abilities and skills. The following passage comes from Exodus 31, where God is giving instructions for building the Temple:

> The Lord spoke to Moses: See, I have called by name Bezalel son of Uri son of Hur, of the tribe of Judah: and I have filled him with divine spirit, with ability, intelligence, and knowledge in every kind of craft, to devise artistic designs, to work in gold, silver, and bronze, in cutting stones for setting, and in carving wood, in every kind of craft. Moreover, I have appointed with him Oholiab son of Ahisamach, of the tribe of Dan; and I have given skill to all the skillful, so that they may make all that I have commanded you: the tent of meeting, and the ark of the covenant, and the mercy seat that is on it, and all the furnishings of the tent, the table and its utensils, and the pure lampstand with all its utensils, and the altar of incense, and the altar of burnt offering with all its utensils, and the basin with its stand, and the finely worked vestments, the holy vestments for the priest Aaron and the vestments of his sons, for their service as priests, and the anointing oil and the fragrant incense for

the holy place. They shall do just as I have commanded you. (vv. 1-11)

Look back at the sequence in this passage. God called Bezalel, and *then* God gave him four things: divine spirit, ability, intelligence, and knowledge. These four gifts had a purpose: They were to enable Bezalel to perform many kinds of crafts that were required for constructing the Temple God had commanded to be built. God also gave a variety of skills to other persons, so they could complete all the tasks needed for the Temple: its physical structure, its furnishings, utensils, and everything down to the garments the priests would wear. As this example shows us, God makes sure those whom God calls to a task have the skills and abilities to perform those tasks. God calls people, and God equips them to fulfill that call.

Let's now think about ways in which skills and abilities can build upon one's effectiveness in the use of a spiritual gift. We will consider a person who has the spiritual gift of teaching and a dream of being a highly effective Bible study leader for adults so that they can know the Word of God and apply its principles to their lives. What skills equip that teacher to do a good job preparing to lead a weekly class and use that gift to its fullest?

1. **Read**—the passage being studied and its placement within the larger narrative (chapter, book, and so on).
2. **Identify**—any unfamiliar words, names, places.
3. **Research**—setting, definitions, pronunciations.
4. **Analyze**—key points in the narrative being studied and note potential applications.
5. **Evaluate**—potential commentaries for additional material.
6. **Consider**—potential questions class members will ask.

7. ***Prepare***—responses to anticipated questions.
8. ***Plan***—questions to ask the class members.
9. ***Organize***—notes for the class session.
10. ***Envision***—the flow of the class session.

While this list could certainly be expanded, we can begin to see just how skills and abilities can equip a spiritual gift to be used most effectively.

Experiences

There is also the common element of including one's life experiences. *Experiences* appears in both the S.H.A.P.E. and S.T.R.I.D.E. models, while it is grouped with Individuality in the G.I.R.D. model. In Shakespeare's play *The Tempest*, one of the characters says, "What's past is prologue."[6] In other words, it's the idea that everything that has gone before has set the stage for what is being experienced in the here and now. This element is important for inclusion because it recognizes all the lessons life has taught each of us—both good and bad—and how those lessons have formed us. The positive experiences are those that we usually think of first as being of the most benefit—the people who have been part of it, the places we've lived or traveled, the jobs we've had, the schools we attended.

The negative experiences in our lives are frequently accompanied by some kind of pain, yet they can often be the most instructive. In Peter's first epistle, he speaks of the new birth into hope given by the resurrection of Jesus: "In this you rejoice, even if now for a little while you have had to suffer various trials, so that the genuineness of your faith—being more precious than gold that, though perishable, is tested by fire—may be found to result in praise and glory and honor when Jesus Christ is revealed" (1 Pet. 1:6-7). Recognizing the experiences of our lives gives us the opportunity to offer praise and glory for all that has gone before. What remains is for us to decide how we reframe our past in ways that continue to imprison us or empower us.

Personality/Individuality

The element of personality or individuality must also be considered as we continue building our profile. While other people will not necessarily learn our life experiences just by spending time with us, personality or individuality traits are the things that others can observe in us. They can see whether we are extroverted or introverted: For example, are we comfortable in a large group of people, or do we prefer to be in a smaller setting? Are we likely to stay in the background, or do we find it a better fit to be in front and in charge? Do we function well with ideas, or do we need specifics? Thinking about our personality elements can enhance our understanding of the experiences of our lives, how our personality shaped our reactions or was shaped by them. All these elements, when considered together, can add further definition as we see ourselves in the fullness of a being created by God.

Occasionally, I learn of people who attended some kind of church ministry training class and, while others enjoyed it and learned something they could use, these few persons said they did not receive any kind of benefit from it. They did not see how or where they would use what was covered and did not experience any kind of motivation to do any further exploration. While there could be a variety of reasons for this, I wonder if the most telling reason they felt that way about the training was that it was for a task that did not correlate in any way to their spiritual gifts. It may not have sparked any part of their personal vision and call and, therefore, offered no inspiration.

As important as it is to know our spiritual gifts, *it is even more important to see them within the larger placement of God's act of giving and equipping toward a purpose.* Equipping must follow gifts, and it must be aligned with those gifts and the intended purpose of their application.

The life experiences, personality/individuality influences, and particular skills we have are helping us refine our spiritual gifts and begin to see the possibilities of fulfilling a vision or dream. They help point to the call God has placed in our lives. We now see how our ministry calling is at the intersection of all these elements. It also affirms how each element contributes to the effectiveness of our servanthood.

As we consider how these elements work together and enhance one another, we must remember God's purpose for the spiritual gifts: They are to be used "for the common good" (see 1 Corinthians 12), meaning the focus is to be outward. As you consider the graphic on page 87, think of it in terms of your congregation: How is God calling your congregation? How is your congregation gifted? What visions are presenting themselves? Does the congregation look at its community—the mission field—and see pain that needs to be alleviated by initiating some kind of ministry or outreach? Now, think cumulatively about all the stories, skills, and personalities

Spiritual Gifts

Personality/
Individuality

Vision

Experiences

Abilities/
Resources

Ministry/Calling

of individuals present in your community of faith. How might the aggregate of these be directed for the common good? We will turn to a corporate version of this application in a later chapter.

CHAPTER SIX

Activating Our Gift-Endowed Potential

His divine power has given us everything needed
for life and godliness, through the knowledge of him
who called us by his own glory and goodness.
—2 PETER 1:3

To each is given the manifestation of
the Spirit for the common good.
—1 CORINTHIANS 12:7

We will now enter the final phase of our development work, that of applying various congregational discipleship models to enable us to fulfill our call through our gifts, vision, resources, personality, and experiences. Hopefully, by now, you realize that employing your spiritual gifts in some form of mission or ministry is not optional when it comes to discipleship; this is what disciples do. This is how we say thank you to God for granting those gifts to us, and it's how we deepen and broaden the arena and impact of our discipleship.

Every local United Methodist Church has the same purpose—that of fulfilling the mission of making disciples of Jesus Christ for the transformation of the world. That mission is realized for each church within the particular context in which that church exists. It affects—and is affected by—the community and its people, which demonstrates a strong bi-directional link between the church and its mission field. The vitality of the congregation is found in how that congregation lives in relationship with its mission field and its members. And, in turn, as the congregation engages in activities to fulfill that mission, it brings its members along on that journey. As the congregation grows stronger in its mission, so does the spirituality of the individual members who engage in that mission.

Within that mission is the system in which the purpose becomes active. That system is a cycle of discipleship that is composed of several elements called the "primary task."[1] It is how we fulfill the mission of the church. The elements of this task are described in paragraph 122 ("The Process for Carrying Out Our Mission") in *The Book of Discipline of The United Methodist Church—2016*:

> We make disciples as we
> — proclaim the gospel, seek, welcome and gather persons into the body of Christ;
> — lead persons to commit their lives to God through baptism by water and the spirit and profession of faith in Jesus Christ;
> — nurture persons in Christian living through worship, the sacraments, spiritual disciplines, and other means of grace, such as Wesley's Christian conferencing;

— send persons into the world to live lovingly and justly as servants of Christ by healing the sick, feeding the hungry, caring for the stranger, freeing the oppressed, being and becoming a compassionate, caring presence, and working to develop social structures that are consistent with the gospel; and

— continue the mission of seeking, welcoming and gathering persons into the community of the body of Christ.

This primary task is at the heart of every church; and, though universal, it is not constrained by context. Rather, it is empowered by context. These processes, when taken in total, create the system by which the church fulfills its mission. While each process can stand alone, its impact is minimal without its connection to the other processes. A healthy congregation continues its cycle of proclaiming, leading, nurturing, and sending. There is no end to the primary task because the mission of the church is perpetual.

Let's examine each part of the primary task more closely.

Proclaim the gospel—When many people hear the word *church*, they think of a building where people congregate on Sunday mornings and various other days of the week for specific activities. The Sunday morning worship service is typically the prime activity of the local church, and much preparation goes into its presentation. It is commonly considered the entry point for church affiliation. In addition to the worship service, the function of proclaiming the gospel is where the community of faith lives out its faith before the world as "living sermons," seeking others without a faith-community relationship. To consider *proclaiming the gospel* to be solely the province of the worship service means that the only persons who will experience this proclamation are those who have brought themselves into the church building for participation in the worship service. It also assumes that proclamation is reserved for the pastor as he or she delivers the sermon.

Both of these depictions are inadequate within the full scope of our call to proclaim the gospel. Proclaiming the gospel is best embodied in the practice of believers as they live and move as disciples of Jesus Christ within their communities. This is where nonbelievers can see an authentic faith in practice. Even while they may drive by the church on Sunday morning and wonder what goes on within its walls, they may recall that one, particular individual in their workplace who lives differently and does so without pressing others to see things his or her way. Or they may recall that certain individual in their fitness class who is always supportive of others' efforts and never voices judgment of anyone. When these memorable individuals are asked "how" and "why," they are not ashamed to declare their faith, and they do so in ways that keep open a possible dialogue that may explore issues of faith and life in greater depth at other times.

The way we gather people into the body of Christ also means we are to receive people where they are and welcome them without assumptions. We live in expectation that we will indeed receive guests in our churches, and we keep our communal life ready to receive our guests. We plan and stay ready to offer our best hospitality—not only social amenities but also what we give of ourselves, our willingness to listen, respecting the pace of entry of our guests. In John 13:34-35, Jesus said, "I give you a new commandment, that you love one another. Just as I have loved you, you also should love one another. By this everyone will know that you are my disciples, if you have love for one another."

Receiving people with openness offers an authentic experience of Christian love. While one would think this would be an easy thing to do, it requires intentional effort. Think about your own congregation on any given Sunday. Scan the sanctuary, the classes, the conversations in the corridors or fellowship hall. Are people engaged in small conversations with only one another or do they also respond to the "strangers" who have entered? Wanting to catch up with our friends on Sundays is understandable, yet, to the guest, those group conversations look like closed relationships that defy entry.

You may notice my use of the word *guest* instead of the more commonly used *visitor*. Keep in mind, *guests* are those you have invited, plan for, look forward to seeing, and whose arrival you anticipate. *Visitors* are the unplanned appearances that frequently interrupt other plans. This distinction may sound inconsequential, but what lies behind it is at the very heart of Christian hospitality: It is with love that we open our doors and invite guests into God's house and make those guests know they are truly welcome. It is not ours to determine their worthiness to enter through those doors; it is ours to extend the saving love of Christ Jesus.

Lead—This is where we connect people with God through baptism and the confession of faith. This point of justifying grace is a momentous step that brings a person into membership in The United Methodist Church and in a local congregation in particular. Baptism begins the work of salvation, and from this point on, the work of sanctifying grace begins. Growing in that grace requires a partnership between the individual and that community of faith. The church introduces people to the practices of the means of grace and supports them as they learn to live those practices. The individual is charged with the mission of beginning to live those practices.

This is the point where formal church membership is entered and vows are made to uphold the church through "prayers, presence, gifts, service, and witness." Many churches offer a new members class that usually includes topics such as the history of the local church, an overview of its governance and operating structure, an introduction of pastoral and lay leadership, highlights of events in the church year, and upcoming calendar opportunities. There also may be a discussion on the membership vows and what they mean.

What is often missing in the new members class is a presentation of that church's intentional process of growing disciples—assuming that local church has such a process—and what the church promises to do to help people become faithful, growing disciples of Christ Jesus. This is where the local church can convey the accountability for growth in discipleship as well as the covenant of support of the congregation and the way the congregation will fulfill its responsibilities in that covenant.

In many cases, in less than a year after a person becomes a member of the local congregation, he or she is added to the membership of a particular committee, board, or team. This is done in the name of assimilating that person into church membership. Yet, shouldn't the issue of membership in that community of faith involve something more than just committee participation?

Nurture—This involves helping people cultivate and practice spiritual disciplines as a pattern of living. This cannot be said enough: While we expect the believer to grow as a disciple, it is the obligation of the church to provide the means, support, and accountability for each person to grow in his or her discipleship. This is the logical follow-up to the above-discussed work of relating someone to God. The task of *nurture* is not a step to achieve and then move on to the next but rather a lifetime role that evolves throughout life. The more deeply we grow, the greater our desire becomes to grow even more. Nurture is how we help one another grow in our discipleship, in sanctifying grace.

The work of nurture is sometimes shortchanged by being viewed as only the task of keeping members of the congregation connected with one another. Common functions of nurture committees include gestures such as sending flowers to a church member who is hospitalized or providing food to a family when there has been a death. This kind of member care is necessary: It is both an expression of hospitality and love. Yet, to *nurture* something means to help it grow.

The work of nurturing the members of the church begins with helping them find their footing as believers and exploring and testing what that means: For example, how well do they know the story of Jesus' and God's unending grace? Do they know how to pray? How do they view the issue of money and personal stewardship? These are just a few of the questions that are at the heart of the ministry of nurturing, and they apply equally to longtime members as much as new believers. Every activity under the banner of *nurture* must answer this question: How has this activity helped the individual grow in ways that enable that person to live a life that reflects Christ?

Send—This means deploying people through training and empowerment for service in the community/mission field. This is another key element in the life of an effective congregation—how well it prepares people to present and represent Christ to those outside its doors through word and deed. The work of *sending* typically involves elements of both outreach and witness, of both compassion and justice making. In outreach, the focus is on those persons beyond the doors of the building, and this may be in the form of responding to an emergency such as a hurricane or flood. It may also take the form of responding to an ongoing need, as some churches participate in programs that provide food and school supplies to children in their communities. The role of the church is to equip people to see the needs and then respond to those needs.

This ministry of outreaching love in action may be directed locally to the community in which that congregation exists. It may also travel beyond that location to state, national, or international needs. When people of faith encounter a system or policies that deprive God's children of justice, they are called to advocate for systems of compassionate justice and righteousness.

Let's look next at ways in which a local congregation could frame an approach to building up the body of Christ.

Membership Vows

When individuals present themselves for membership in a local congregation of The United Methodist Church, they are presented with a vow to uphold the church by their prayers, presence, gifts, service, and witness. Then, in the worship service, the pastor turns to the congregation and asks them to reaffirm their covenant for the same. This mutuality is at the heart of formational discipleship. It speaks to the individuals' willingness to begin a journey of growth, and it holds the congregation's members accountable for helping those persons on their journey while promising to continue their own journey.

Prayers

We keep the community of faith, its people, its ministries (both current and emerging), and its mission field in our prayers, praising

God for what we have and asking God to keep the church in line with God's desires for that church in that particular community. Our prayers should also include a request for God to reveal to us the ways in which God calls us to bear witness to the gospel of Jesus Christ as we discern and seek to fulfill our call to ministry.

Presence

Our vow of presence is typically presented as meaning our commitment to attendance at church services, celebrating God's abundant grace and the Resurrection promise of Christ Jesus. It could also be interpreted as our willingness to be present with others in the community of faith, offering a comforting hand or a listening ear to someone in need or despair. That offering, in turn, should flow outward to those in our mission field, the people in our community.

One location where I worked was an executive suite of offices that had a communal coffee station in an anteroom. On one particular morning, I had gone for coffee and saw one of my fellow employees getting a cup, so I greeted her, "How are you today?" She immediately began ticking off everything she had scheduled for that day and the various meetings and projects she was responsible for and how far behind she felt on many of them. I stopped her and said, "I didn't ask about your schedule; I asked about *you.*" Tears began to well up in her eyes, and she replied, "Thank you. No one ever asks me that." This small offering of presence made a difference for her and was a reminder for me that some of our greatest offerings of presence can come in the smallest moments, and this requires our being fully aware of what is said and what is expressed without words. We need to learn to "hear between the lines." I was reminded that fulfilling God's call is not relegated to large acts; practicing even such a small act of presence is a response to God.

Gifts

When we covenant to uphold the church with our gifts, we are committing both to offering our financial resources and to the sharing of our spiritual gifts. Our views toward and practice of sharing our financial resources are an expression of our priorities of discipleship, much like praying and reading the Bible. It is an expression of our trust in God to sustain us in all our needs, as God sustained the Israelites with manna.

Offering our spiritual gifts requires us to know what those gifts are and how best to deploy them, both personally and for the congregation as a whole. Pledging to use our gifts connects us to the passage in Ephesians 4:12 that states the purpose: to build up the body of Christ. Using our gifts calls for our engagement within a collaborative, cooperative, and connected community of believers. (Later, we will address the role spiritual gifts can take in a formal system of leadership development.)

However, it bears noting that at the point of taking these vows of membership, it is highly likely that the only understanding one will have of "gifts" is from a financial perspective. In order for a new member to fulfill all the meanings of *gifts*, the congregation's leadership is automatically obligated to offer some means to each one to discover what his or her spiritual gifts may be. Without that, we relegate the vow of upholding the congregation with our gifts to be narrowly construed as dealing only with money.

Service

Our *service* is just that—how we can offer our time and talents for the activities of ministry in the congregation and beyond. Remember, the membership vows apply both to the internal life and to the external life of the church in the community and elsewhere. This is one of the advantages of being in a connectional church such as The United Methodist Church—membership in one local church connects us with membership in all other United Methodist congregations. Our *service* usually will involve our helping on some ministry project or activity, according to our spiritual gifts, our available time, and our interests. Occasionally, though, our church may need us to help with something that doesn't exactly align with our interests, gifts, or abilities. In such instances, it may be tempting to respond, "That doesn't work with my gifts" and then turn down the request for assistance—but that is not who God is calling us to be. Such a request is not an imposition; rather, it is an opportunity to fulfill a vow to offer service when the church needs help and to do so with a generous heart.

North Carolina has a professional hockey team called the Carolina Hurricanes, and one night, when they were playing the Toronto Maple Leafs, misfortune struck. The Hurricanes' goalie was injured and had to come out of the game. They called in the reserve goalie, but he too was soon injured and had to leave the game. The Hurricanes needed a goalie, but there wasn't another one on the bench. The coach then realized the arena had an employee in the building who sometimes played goalie during practice sessions. This man was eligible to serve as a backup goalie, but he had never played in an NHL game. And besides, he already had a job to do that night: He was the Zamboni driver, tasked with clearing and resurfacing the ice during the game, between each period. The Hurricanes called him in to play, and he suited up for them. He started off roughly, getting scored on with the first two shots he faced; but eventually, he would go on to stop eight shots on goal that night, and he helped the Hurricanes win the game 6-3.[2] The moral of the story? Sometimes, when the team needs help, it's time to get off the Zamboni, get in the game, and help them.

Witness

Witness was added to the church membership vows only recently because it had become too easy for individuals to be involved in all aspects of their church's life without connecting that activity with Christ and sharing Christ with those around them.[3] Far too many people still do not know how to articulate the journey of their faith and tell that story to someone else so that Christ may be revealed.

The very word *evangelism* seems to cause anxiety among some people, based on any number of reasons. Ironically, some of this anxiety may be due to evangelism's being listed as a spiritual gift, and if people do not possess that gift to any degree, they may feel the obligation to share the faith doesn't apply to them. And perhaps some of the anxiety over the idea of evangelism may be due to feelings of inadequacy about one's own faith. Some people may think that if they start sharing their faith with an unchurched person, they will be barraged with a number of questions they cannot answer, so they don't say anything.

Fulfilling our vow to witness has a wide range of possibilities that all begin with being honest about who we are—our successes and failures, what God has done in our lives, and why life with Jesus is better than life without him.

The General Rule of Discipleship

In the early days of Methodism, John Wesley realized that people needed to know and experience God's love and grace and that the best way to do that was within a supportive community. Thus, the class meeting system was born, and in these small groups of a dozen people, a designated leader would guide the members through a formational process that not only educated them but also influenced people toward living into Christlike behaviors. The General Rules of the Wesleyan movement provided the format and structure for these class meetings, and they became a transformative hallmark of Methodism. Though time has passed and the world has changed, Methodists remain a people committed to loving God and loving others in both public and private ways.

While the basic purpose remains the same, these class meeting groups are now known as covenant discipleship groups. Their underlying structure is found in the principles expressed in Matthew 22:37-40, which is known as "The Great Commandment." Within this passage, we find two basic commands: Love God and love others. Our love of God is expressed both publicly, through our participation in and with a worshiping community; and privately, through our personal time with God. The acts of worship and devotion are termed "works of piety."

The second command of loving others is also expressed both privately, through our acts of compassion as we discover the needs of others; and publicly, through our work of confronting systems that are unjust. These acts of compassion and justice making are termed "works of mercy." Together, the commitment to both works of piety and works of mercy form the General Rule of Discipleship. The balance between the two is crucial to healthy discipleship: To focus only on our worship experiences but never respond to the preached Word of God in tangible ways is selfish; to confront unjust systems without spiritual grounding risks action without direction.

How might we use the General Rule of Discipleship to more fully develop our opportunities to use our gifts? First, let us remember that the elements of the rule are complementary. The public and private expressions of our faith need each other. It is the same with the works of mercy and works of piety. To practice from only one expression and not the other lessens our abilities to learn and practice discipleship. These relationships can also be explored in a cross pattern. For example, how does our practice of worship (public piety) impact our compassion (private mercy), and how do our acts of compassion impact our experience of worship? What can our devotional life practices (private piety) inspire for justice making (public mercy), and how do our acts of justice-making impact our practice of devotion?

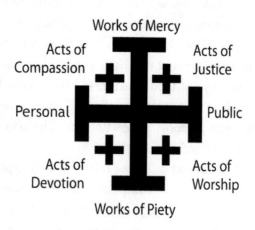

Works of Mercy

Acts of Compassion — Acts of Justice

Personal — Public

Acts of Devotion — Acts of Worship

Works of Piety

Exploring these interdependent relationships can open up new understandings of how God works in our lives, drawing us closer in our relationships with God and with others and showing us how God calls us to use those deepening relationships as a springboard for action.

In his sermon number 92, "On Zeal," John Wesley addressed the purpose of the church. He began by describing the state of the individual—that of possessing and living out a love of God and others, a love that had no equal. This love flowed from the fruit of the Spirit, and it, in turn, was manifested in individuals living out the works of mercy. The works of piety are those spiritual disciplines that compel an individual to practice the works of mercy. All of this, Wesley concluded, was gathered by God into every local church.[4]

Reversing this narrative offers a model for growing disciples. People enter the church, and the church then teaches people to live the works of piety (means of grace/spiritual disciplines). As people engage in those practices, they find motivation to practice works of mercy (feeding those who are hungry, caring for those who are poor, and so on). Adopting these activities into a lifestyle produces a life marked by the fruit of the spirit. When we live from that fruit, it becomes clear that our love of God and others defines our lives in every facet, and everything else falls short.

What these models hold in common is their *intentionality*. Each design and each component within that design is there for a reason. Each stage also leads to the next and is dependent upon the previous stage. By employing such models, independently or simultaneously, local churches can eliminate the haphazardness and provide the means by which people can grow in their faith. They become transformed people who can transform the world.

Gathering our gifts, dreams, resources, and experiences within our call paints an image of how our discipleship can be formed and lived out. By applying that wholeness within the cycle of discipleship (the primary task), we can find places where our ministry contributes to the methods by which the church fulfills its mission. It is interesting to consider where our gifts find a natural alignment. For example, the gift of shepherding may fit well within the task of nurture. The gift of evangelism may fit well with the instruction to gather. This helps us see how our individual calls contribute to the overall mission of the church. As with the body metaphor the apostle Paul cited, each individual element of the whole is necessary. This process of linking gifts can also be applied to the membership vows. Shepherding could align with *presence*, and evangelism could align with *witness*.

Intentional methods that enable a local church to fulfill its mission—making disciples of Jesus Christ for the transformation of the world—provide the places where a called and gifted disciple can contribute to that mission and experience spiritual growth in the process. In the next and final chapter, we will look at suggestions for how a local church can make gift identification and development a vital part of how the church fulfills its mission.

CHAPTER 7

Increasing the Impact

I long to see you so that I may impart to you some
spiritual gift to make you strong—that is, that you and
I may be mutually encouraged by each other's faith.

—ROMANS 1:11-12, NIV

To know your own spiritual gifts is both important and helpful for discerning and responding to ministry opportunities. It can bring a sense of peace in knowing there is a deep spiritual connection between who you are as a created and gifted child of God and how God may be calling you to live for Christ. It can also offer a sense of relief to realize there are some places of discipleship service that work better than others.

As shared earlier, people are occasionally requested to step in and help with an event or program that needs more help than anyone had envisioned. These are the folks who "get off the Zamboni" and agree to offer a brief time of service; they are neither being asked, nor are they agreeing to, a permanent assignment. However, there are also people whose good nature, sense of obligation, and/

or occasional inability to say "no" lead to their serving on a committee, even though this particular area doesn't appeal to their interests. They struggle to feel as though their efforts make any kind of difference; and, ultimately, they feel they have failed at their task. As a result, the person loses the desire to serve, and church leaders may consider that individual as not having much to contribute in general, based upon previous efforts. Ultimately, the church loses the connection with that individual as a disciple desiring to serve Christ. Yet, has the individual failed, or has the system that placed that person in those roles failed?

There is an important axiom in the field of systems thinking: Every system is perfectly designed for the results it produces. Therefore, if the results are not what is desired, first fix the system and then the people. Throughout my working life, I have seen numerous examples of this adage being ignored. In such situations I've observed, a highly effective person would be placed in a job because other people kept failing at achieving the desired results. Yet, that star performer did not produce the star results he or she was expected to produce. Why? Because the system into which that person was placed was faulty and anyone placed in it would fail on some level, if not on all levels.

Be advised, though, that it is not sufficient to try to "fix" the part of the system we believe is failing. If one part is failing, the entire system is failing. To focus on only one element without understanding how that one part affects all the others—and is affected by all the others—is called suboptimization. This approach does not fix a bad system; it merely creates a different failed system, with the cause of its failure now lying somewhere else.

Consider this example: You realize one day that your arms do not have much strength, so you decide to begin weight training to correct the problem. You enroll in a local weight-training class, and you are told from the outset, "Always work opposing muscles. If you work the biceps, you must also work the triceps." This is because these opposing muscles function together as a "system." This system must be addressed as a whole to allow for proper muscle development and to enable the training to achieve its maximum impact and support overall health. Working only the biceps would be an example of suboptimization—working a part of the system without addressing the whole. One muscle is developed, while its opposing muscle is underdeveloped and, ultimately, weakened. Consider too that this two-muscle system of biceps and triceps is also part of a larger system, the muscular system of the human body.

In 1 Corinthians 12, Paul uses the same metaphor in speaking of the role of spiritual gifts in relation to the body of Christ, the worshiping community. While Paul had never heard of "systems thinking," he explains its principles very well. He first sets the stage by establishing that there is but one source of gifts, services, and activities (vv. 4-6). He goes on to address the need for the diversity and the endowment of those gifts, services, and activities, all while reemphasizing the singularity of their source. Paul then compares this diverse endowment of gifts to the human body and underscores the need for all parts—and for each of those parts—to perform the function for which they were designed. Without that, the body cannot function. And so it is with the body of Christ.

As good as it may be for us as individuals to understand our own gifts, it would be like only one part of the body knowing what it is supposed to do. In the scenario above, it would be like one muscle becoming strong while the opposing muscle remains weak. In a local congregation, this would appear as a few members functioning from wholeness and the rest receiving no attention or care and left to fend for themselves spiritually. Instead, Paul says, "Each of us should please our neighbors for their good, to build them up" (Rom. 15:2, NIV).

What would it be like if all leaders in a local church knew their gift picture and where it may be pointing them to live out their discipleship? What would it look like to use spiritual gifts in our local churches as the basis for a system of identifying and recruiting people into various leadership roles? This system would offer ways of bringing order to the annual task of determining the leadership of the boards and committees of each local church. There would also be a bonus: It could help launch new ministries that respond to the emerging needs of the mission field of the local church.

Local United Methodist congregations are challenged each year with the often overwhelming task of identifying ministry leaders for the congregation. They usually do this in the late summer and early autumn as the committee on nominations and leadership development meets to consider its seasonal task of nominating persons for the various responsibilities in the congregation.

> There shall be elected annually, by the charge conference in each local church, a committee on nominations and leadership development that is composed of professing members of the local church. The charge of this committee is to identify, develop, deploy, evaluate, and monitor Christian spiritual leadership for the local congregation. Members of the committee shall engage in and be attentive to developing and enhancing their own Christian spiritual life in light of the mission of the Church (Part VI, Chapter One, Section 1).

In conducting its work, the committee shall engage
in biblical and theological reflections on the mission of
the church, the primary task, and ministries of the local
church. It shall provide a means of identifying the spiritual gifts and abilities of the membership. The committee
shall work with the church council, or alternative administrative bodies, to determine the diverse ministry tasks
of the congregation and the skills needed for leadership.

(¶258.1, *The Book of Discipline of*
The United Methodist Church—2016)

The first task of the committee on nominations and leadership
development is to stay faithful to the biblical and theological principles of servant leadership as the committee provides guidance to
the operating structures of the local church. The committee's members are challenged to continue the development of their own spirituality as they perform their responsibilities. This tells us that this
committee should meet frequently throughout the year, yet many
local church committees on nominations and leadership development meet only during nominations season to prepare for leadership transitions and the annual charge conference.

Second, they are to complete the job of finding people to
assume leadership roles for the congregation and its various ministries by using spiritual gifts and assessing the skills of members
of the church. This is where the individual process outlined in this
book could be applied. If you are currently serving on a committee or team in your church, imagine what that group would be like
and how its functioning would be affected by each person knowing his or her spiritual gifts as well as being united in a common

hope for how all members may share and serve Christ through that committee.

A third task is the cooperative work of determining what ministries are needed both within the church and beyond its doors in the mission field of that community. And, while we have latitude for creating customized ministries, we still have obligations for certain ministry tasks that are designed to ensure justice, oversight, and the prudent management of the local church. A common challenge these committees face is that of eliminating or minimizing the burnout that occurs from people who try to do too much for too long or who try to do something that doesn't engage their hearts and passions.

Perhaps we need to consider different questions in the life and work of this important committee. Rather than ask who could do which job, the committee on nominations and leadership development members need to reframe their task by asking themselves these two questions:

1. What is our system for identifying persons for leadership and service in our church? Is our system producing the results we desire?
2. If we are not seeing the results we desire, how do we change the system?

Values of an Effective Gifts-Based Ministry System

Before we move into the technical aspects of initiating a gifts-based system or improving an existing one, let's consider the principles of such a system. What makes for an effective system of gifts-based ministry deployment? Keep in mind, this system includes not only the discovery of spiritual gifts but also other elements that point someone to a particular ministry: personal skills and abilities, a vision for making a difference for someone or for some condition, and personal experiences. Since the heart of gifts-based ministry relies on the alignment of people, gifts, and the ministries of the church, we will explore these values within the context of the committee on nominations and leadership development in the local church.

First, an effective system is one whose purpose is scriptural: "The gifts he gave were that some would be apostles, some prophets, some evangelists, some pastors and teachers, to equip the saints for the work of ministry, for building up the body of Christ" (Eph. 4:11-12). Paul's words remind us that there is but one reason the gifts are given, and that is for the purpose of growing the health of the church. A healthy church is one that fulfills its biblical mandates, reaching out to all within its reach. It is one in which its people live their lives as disciples who, by following the example of Christ, offer daily testimony to God's presence and saving grace in their lives.

In First Corinthians, Paul's stated purpose for using spiritual gifts was that they be directed "for the common good" (12:7); and in Romans, he emphasized unity. Taken together, these verses point to the employment of spiritual gifts as essential to a healthy, functioning, Christlike community of believers. To frame this within the language of the stated mission of The United Methodist Church, this is a picture of "transformed" believers working for "the transformation of the world."

A second value of an effective system is the presence of supportive leadership, both clergy and laity. A key objective of leadership is to equip others to do ministry. In United Methodist polity, the pastor is the chairperson of the committee on nominations and leadership development (¶258.1c, *Book of Discipline*), and the work of the committee is shared with a number of laypersons. Church leaders function within a community of leaders, a community that should be cooperative, collaborative, and supportive of one another. Clarity of ministry expectations is a big step required to achieve this, and leaders who help one another function at their very best are the component that makes it work. We speak of empowering people for ministry; but often, we fail to *equip* them (teach or train them with the necessary skills and knowledge) to perform the ministry before we *empower* them (conveying to them the authority), and they then fall short of the expectations that were placed upon them. By not focusing on the equipping of persons for leadership, in both the task specifics and the roles and approach of leadership in general, we effectively set them up for failure.

A third value is this: A gifts-based approach is integrated into all the ministries of the local church. It is not a single program ministry, operating on its own; instead, it is the way all ministries are done. In fulfilling its responsibilities, the committee on nominations and leadership development is to consider the church's leadership needs in light of the ministries of the church. Special attention needs to be paid to the ministries of outreach and evangelism, as they connect the congregation to its community—its mission field. Paul's words are important to remember here, as he spoke to the purpose of the spiritual gifts: "To each is given the manifestation of the Spirit for the common good" (1 Cor. 12:7).

However you design your own spiritual gifts-based system, keep these values in mind, as they will offer a firm foundation for a workable process. They will also be timeless enough that they can withstand most any changes the congregation may face.

We cannot forget that sanctifying grace is the process by which people grow in their knowledge of and obedience to Christ's teachings. That growth can come through service as we relate to other members of God's family. It can also come through the deepening practices of spiritual disciplines and through accountable relationships that promote self-reflection and continual discernment of the person God calls each of us to be.

The Fifth *W*

Whenever we take on any kind of project activity, whether it's in ministry or in a secular environment, we deal with the "five *W*s and an *H*." Answering *Who*, *What*, *Where*, *When*, and *How* can paint a fairly clear picture of the project, and it communicates to all what their job is and the deadlines, resources, and partners necessary for fulfilling their role. However, one *W* is usually ignored: the *Why*. We don't pay much attention to it because we often assume other people know the answer to that question; however, very often, people do not. (There is a video on YouTube that does a great job of explaining the power of "why." It is a TED talk by Simon Sinek titled "Start with Why." If you have online access, it is worth the time to watch it.)

Dr. W. Edwards Deming, an expert in statistical process control, frequently spoke about the relationship between quality job performance and an individual's full understanding of the purpose of any particular assigned task. Though I never got to attend one of his workshops in person, I recall watching a video of part of his presentation. In one example, he described the need for clear communication of the larger purpose of any given task and, therefore, the expectations for how that task should be carried out. Very often, if someone fails at an assignment, it may not have been the person's fault. Dr. Deming preached that good employees could not overcome bad systems. Knowing the expectations for any task, he maintained, would help people do the job with better results.

Imagine telling someone to clean a large, flat board. That person does so; but without knowing how that board will be used, the individual is left to guess what methods to use—and if that guess is wrong, the task may need to be done again. On the other hand, if a person is told to clean that same board so that food could be prepared on it, the individual now has a more precise idea of the kind of cleaning effort that must be exerted, the tools necessary to accomplish the task, and the degree of standards that must be met to complete the task to satisfaction. There is now no guessing at the necessary methods, and the task can be completed with a sense of accomplishment.

Without a clear purpose—the *Why*—any effort will do. Knowing the *why* equips us to aim our efforts at the reason that ministry exists and to know how its effectiveness will be assessed. It points to the vision for that ministry effort and can describe what the vision will look like when realized. It also carries the expectations of the degree of human effort needed to achieve its fulfillment, and it points to the kind of activities that will be engaged in the pursuit of that purpose.

For example, which of the following ministry job descriptions would be more spiritually fulfilling to serve?

1. A committee with responsibilities for the supervision and care of church assets and acquired property and with oversight responsibilities for the church's insurance; or

2. A committee responsible for the care and upkeep of all aspects of the church property so members and guests alike can experience a clean, safe, and inviting environment in which to worship God and participate in the church's fellowship and ministries.

With both descriptions, it's the same committee, with the same responsibilities. The difference lies in the *why*. In the second description, the word *so* points to the spiritual reason that particular committee exists. For the disciple, it is more satisfying to be engaged in something that points people to God rather than activities that do not.

A friend of mine was coaching a congregation and its members in their revitalization effort. At one session, they were describing the various ministries the congregation engaged in during a typical year. As each activity was described, the coach posted it on a flipchart and then asked them why they did that particular ministry: What is its purpose? One of those ministries was an autumn festival, and the group members talked about all the work required in getting it ready. They struggled to express why they did it. Finally, one individual said, "We do it to raise enough money to pay our apportionments." All agreed on this as the sole reason for the event. Clearly, this was not their favorite ministry activity, but it enabled them to meet their annual financial obligations.

The coach then explained how their apportionments were used in a way that enabled them to be in mission and ministry around the world. This congregation's dollars joined those of all other congregations, thereby multiplying their reach far beyond their capabilities as a single church. He shared how the monies were used to address the priorities of the denomination and affect the lives of everyday people in a positive manner. Apportionments enabled them to help raise up lay and clergy leaders around the world and plant new congregations far and wide. Apportionments also supported ministries with the poor and addressed issues of global health. The coach reminded them that his work with them came free of charge because their apportionment dollars helped make that possible.

After some discussion, the congregation members began seeing how their festival event was not simply a fundraising activity but rather one that could enable them to change the lives of people they would never meet, people who were beloved children of God and for whom Jesus died.

There is an often-told story of an architect who is hired to rebuild a cathedral that had been destroyed by fire. When visiting the site one day, the architect comes upon three bricklayers. He asks each one what he is doing. The first one says he is laying bricks to make money to support his family. The second one says he is building a wall. The third bricklayer says he is building a cathedral. Each man is performing the same repetitive task. But the difference is in the perception each man has of his role within the larger project and the contribution his own work makes. The first two are focused on the immediacy of the task. However, the third man sees the *why*, and he is able to connect his menial task to the larger vision.

Think about your own involvement in your church. If you are working with a particular ministry, does that ministry have a clear purpose statement? If not, what would it be? How does that particular ministry help people grow in spiritual maturity and in the knowledge and love of Jesus and his call to discipleship? If a clear purpose statement cannot be determined, then the obvious question is, Why are we doing this ministry?

- *Why do we offer Bible study classes?* "We offer Bible study classes so people can learn about God's love and grace and encounter Jesus as Savior."
- *Why do we have a music ministry?* "We have a music ministry so people can experience praising God through song and so that the worship setting can minister to people through sound."

The responses to the question you pose should point to the reason for doing that particular ministry, and that reason should point to God. Having clear purpose (*Why*) statements for each ministry also helps people determine the best allocation of resources. If we cannot determine a clear reason for a particular ministry, we need to consider ways to make it more clearly connected to the mission of the church or consider eliminating it.

System Implementation Process

Where does one begin to transform a system? What steps do we need to follow? How long will it take? These questions and others are the questions church leaders need to ask as they transition to a leadership development and deployment system that is based on spiritual gifts. What follows are some general steps for a church committee on nominations and leadership development to use in making this transition—and these can be adapted, depending upon the uniqueness of one's own local church.

Step 1: Choose a spiritual gifts-assessment instrument to use. Make sure it is user friendly and fits the culture and context of your congregation. Consider how easy it will be to track data and determine what means will be used to track that data. Become familiar with the assessment tool you choose.

Documents should be easy to read and instructions clearly understood. A tracking system for data is essential, but it does not need to be complicated. If computer spreadsheets work for your church, great. If 3- x 5-inch index cards in a shoebox better suit your style, that will also work. Just keep in mind that if any part of your system is confusing, difficult to understand, or unwieldy to use, the entire system will fail.

Step 2: Work with members of the committee on nominations to help them discover their own spiritual gifts and to become conversant in the language of the process and the meanings of the gifts. Make sure they are clear on steps to take related to their responsibilities. To use spiritual gifts as a means of identifying potential leaders requires that those who use the assessment tool must first understand it and know how to use it.

Step 3: Develop spiritual gifts profiles with the current ministry and committee leaders and members; begin with what you currently have. This step will be of great benefit in broadening the base of understanding of spiritual gifts-based ministry and in subsequent steps in your process. Be prepared, though: People may discover that their gifts and interests do not truly lie within the ministry in which they are serving. Provide an opportunity for people to disengage from a ministry if they feel better suited for another; these may be the very people who said "yes" out of a sense of obligation, and offering them the opportunity to make a change can mean the difference between joyful service and burnout.

Step 4: Develop ministry descriptions for all current ministries. A ministry description is comparable to a job description. This one-page document describes the purpose of a particular ministry and specific elements of that ministry. That purpose statement must give a clear picture of the exact reasons the ministry exists. It must accurately describe the *What, How, When, Where, Who,* and *Why* of that ministry. Consider this an opportunity to state the "God reason" the ministry exists. Make sure the "why" statements are clear and compelling. Remember that "Because we've always done it" is not a good answer to the question "Why?"

In addition, a ministry description should include a naming of the spiritual gifts that are helpful to have (yet never mandatory); skills and abilities that are helpful; and general information, such as the number of hours required or expected, the name of the ministry chairperson/leader, and that person's contact information. (This is a great task for the existing ministry teams/committees to perform and complete, and it is why we had them go through the process in Step 3.)

Step 5: Set up and test the data-tracking system and begin tracking the data of all persons who previously completed gifts profiles. Train more than one person in using your chosen system, as it is always helpful to have a backup. Be sure to cross-reference spiritual gifts and dreams with names. It will help both with current ministries and in the creation of new ministries.

Step 6: Set a realistic implementation schedule. Save yourself the frustration that comes with unmet deadlines and promises that cannot be delivered because the rollout schedule is far too ambitious. Just focus on working through the process to the best of your ability; it is best to start small and grow as you go.

Consider adopting a "guest committee member" approach to participation. Granted, we designate formal leaders annually, so why not consider allowing non-committee members to drop in on a meeting of ministry that interests them? Such openness allows people to be affirmed as ministers and realize that the priesthood of all believers is real and functioning. The system must be open and accessible to people as they seek to find their rightful place of ministry in God's church. This fluidity also offers an environment into which new ministries can be birthed and in which ministries that no longer serve a need can be reframed or brought to a conclusion.

What About Creating New Ministries?

Working from a spiritual gifts-based perspective offers a helpful structure for launching new ministries. By starting with a particular spiritual gift and then considering the particular passions, motivations, or areas of interest of people who have that gift, the church can expand its reach into their mission field. For example, let's start with several people who all have the gift of teaching in your local church, yet each one has a different interest area. What would that look like?

- Yuko has a passion for ministering to people in extended-care settings. She begins teaching Bible studies in an assisted-living facility.
- Mateo has a passion for organic gardening. He begins teaching organic gardening techniques in a community garden set up by his local church.
- Jasmine has an interest in photography. She begins teaching a photography class to teens at a local youth center.
- Barry continues to celebrate getting out of debt. He decides to apply his gift of teaching to lead classes that help others get out from under the burden of personal debt.

Looking over those examples, we see four ministries that use the gift of teaching, yet none of them involves teaching a Sunday school class.

Now, let's look at the possibilities when we start with people who have motivation for the same social issue: kids who come home to an empty house.

- Ellen has the gift of administration. She uses it to organize an afterschool program that offers tutoring for children, help with their homework, and healthy snacks.
- Francisco has the gift of leadership. He uses it to tell the story of the program and reach out to enlist volunteers.
- Jada has the gift of giving. She not only creates a fundraising campaign, she also makes a significant contribution to get it going.
- Bruce has the gift of faith. He uses it to organize prayer teams to undergird the program, the children it serves, and the volunteers who staff it.

That is how we can apply a variety of spiritual gifts to a shared passion or dream. In these examples, each person is serving out of his or her particular gifts and doing something he or she cares about very deeply.

This kind of approach also frees us from believing that supporting gifts aren't needed for upfront ministries. Consider the following example: Carrie loves the music ministry at her church and would love to be part of the choir. There is a problem, though: Carrie cannot sing. She has tried, but she has resorted just to mouthing the words when the congregation joins in singing a hymn. But Carrie *does* have the gifts of administration and serving. So, in July, when the announcement was made that the choir was going to present a

Christmas madrigal festival, fully staged with costumes and props, Carrie knew where she could help. She happily volunteered to organize the costume crew and produce all the costumes needed for the festival. As the madrigal performance was offered, she stood behind the curtain and heard all the oohs and aahs when the spotlight came up on the costumed choir. Carrie's gift-based ministry made a difference, even though she never took the spotlight herself, and that was fine with her.

These are elements of a spiritual gifts-based system of leader identification, development, and ministry. It is a year-round process that is flexible enough to respond to emerging issues that affect the church and the community the church serves.

Let us be candid in saying the transformation to a spiritual gifts-based system is neither quick nor easy. It is, however, worth the effort. Helping people discover their spiritual gifts and connecting them with their call and their God-given abilities enables them to truly reflect Christ as they strive for the common good. It is the body of Christ fulfilling the mission of the church.

A Few Final Words

About twenty years ago, I had the opportunity to join a multiday retreat model that equipped the participants to reflect upon their call and then put words to it. It was a deep self-examination with time for scriptural reflection; a personal analysis of one's life and ministry roles and values; and, ultimately, an iteration of one's vision. Within that, I could discover all those instances that gave me the thrill and joy of being in the right place at the right time. Those were the occasions that revealed my passion and enthusiasm for service. Then, when I applied the lens of my own spiritual gifts,

I saw all the ways, both big and small, in which God had equipped me to respond to those opportunities. Each instance had given me the chance to use my gifts and further develop them through my work. The compilation of all this resulted in what was called a "personal calling statement." What that opportunity afforded me was the chance to look at all the ways in which I had found a hint of something being evoked in my being—things throughout my life that, when considered as a whole, offered a pattern that I could identify only as my calling. Not all of them were positive experiences, but even the negatives can become positives when they are viewed as educational. God certainly let me try several paths; yet, each time, God lovingly pulled me back closer to the road I was to walk. Putting this into words offered a path for life and ministry that has made a difference in my life and, I pray, in the lives of others.

This journey into spiritual gifts offers joyous discoveries that enhance our discipleship and help us live closer to God. Discovering and serving from our spiritual gifts offers us the opportunity to focus on all that God has given each of us and to thank God by using those gifts in furtherance of living our call to ministry as baptized believers. As we consider those gifts, we ask ourselves how we can use them. That is where God has planted a spark in our heart, a spark that is ignited when we encounter people or issues we believe are in need of our help and work. That vision presents a goal, a picture of what could be, and engages the emotions. When serving through that personal vision, we find energy, motivation, and satisfaction.

Assessing our gifts and vision, we realize that we also have a number of resources at our disposal. The skills and abilities we possess enable us to serve with effectiveness in whatever role we take. Our lives offer great lessons that we can apply to our chosen area of service. The experiences that have shaped us can often be used in our ministry, and how we respond to life's situations is largely tempered by our personality traits. All these elements make each of us unique—the unique individuals God created us to be. Let us give praise for that.

As a community of faith gathers to proclaim the gospel, to relate people to God through membership and the sacraments, to nurture one another as they grow in sanctifying grace, and to send them into the world as transformed people who can transform the world, we recognize the tremendous opportunity God offers us and the need to formalize the individual processes into a system that can provide internal support and encouragement. Let us go forth with Paul's words in our hearts: "Like good stewards of the manifold grace of God, serve one another with whatever gift each of you has received" (1 Pet. 4:10).

NOTES

Chapter One: Why Spiritual Gifts?

1. Kenneth Cain Kinghom, *Discovering Your Spiritual Gifts: A Personal Inventory Method* (Grand Rapids, MI: Zondervan, 1981), 8.
2. Sandy Jackson with Brian Jackson, *Lay Servant Ministries: Basic Course Participant's Book* (Nashville, TN: Discipleship Resources, 2017), 16–17.

Chapter Four: The Calling of the Saints

1. Quote Investigator, "Sports Do Not Build Character; They Reveal It: John Wooden? Heywood Hale Broun? James Michener? Anonymous?," https://quoteinvestigator.com/2015/04/08/sports/#more-10936.
2. Colton Gardner, "Self-Storage Industry Statistics (2020)," neighbor.com (December 18, 2019), https://www.neighbor.com/storage-blog/self-storage-industry-statistics/.
3. Save the Children, "Food Insecurity in America Is Cutting Childhoods Short," https://www.savethechildren.org/us/charity-stories/food-insecurity-america-malnutrition-united-states.

Chapter Five: Expanding Our Profile

1. Rick Warren, *The Purpose Driven Church: Every Church Is Big in God's Eyes* (Grand Rapids, MI: Zondervan, 1995), 370–75.
2. Carol Cartmill and Yvonne Gentile, *Serving from the Heart: Finding Your Gifts and Talents for Service*, Updated Edition (Nashville, TN: Abingdon Press, 2011), 12, 37–42.

3. G.I.R.D. model created by and copyright © the Connectional Ministries staff of the North Carolina Annual Conference of The United Methodist Church. Used with permission. All rights reserved.
4. Alis Alberta career planning website, https://alis.alberta.ca/career insite/know-yourself/skills-quiz/.
5. Abilities and skills list compiled based upon lists from the Alis Alberta career planning website, https://alis.alberta.ca/careerinsite/knowy-ourself/skills-quiz/; and William R. Tracey, Designing Training and Development Systems (New York: AMACOM, 1992), 205.
6. William Shakespeare, *The Tempest*, act 2, scene 1, line 253.

Chapter Six: Activating Our Gift-Endowed Potential

1. *The Book of Discipline of The United Methodist Church—2016* (Nashville, TN: The United Methodist Publishing House, 2016), ¶¶ 243, 258.1.
2. Emily Kaplan, "Zamboni Driver, 42, Stars as Emergency Goalie for Hurricanes," espn.com (February 22, 2020), https://www.espn.com/nhl/story/_/id/28761372/zamboni-driver-42-stars-emergency-goalie-hurricanes.
3. Julie Dwyer, "What It Means to Witness: Honoring Our United Methodist Vow," umc.org (October 6, 2017), https://www.umc.org/en/content/what-it-means-to-witness-honoring-our-united-methodist-vow.
4. John Wesley, Sermon 92, "On Zeal," §II.5, in *Sermons III*, 3:313.

ANSWER KEY FOR
SPIRITUAL GIFTS INVENTORY

Group A	Healing
Group B	Discernment
Group C	Serving
Group D	Tongues
Group E	Teaching
Group F	Apostleship
Group G	Giving
Group H	Faith
Group I	Interpretation of Tongues
Group J	Prophecy
Group K	Wisdom
Group L	Leadership
Group M	Evangelism
Group N	Compassion/Mercy
Group O	Administration
Group P	Working Miracles
Group Q	Knowledge
Group R	Shepherding
Group S	Helps
Group T	Exhortation

Printed in the USA
CPSIA information can be obtained
at www.ICGtesting.com
LVHW020746111023
760325LV00008B/16